The Wandering Beloved

DAVID SMALL

The Wandering Beloved

THE WANDERING BELOVED

Copyright © 2015, 2025 David Small.

Small Revolution Publishing

ISBN (Paperback): 978-0-9917724-4-5

ISBN (Hardcover): 978-0-9917724-6-9

ISBN (eBook): 978-0-9917724-5-2

Written by: David Small Edited by: Elizabeth Ridley

All rights reserved. No part of this book may be used or reproduced by any means, graphic, electronic, or mechanical, including photocopying, recording, taping or by any information storage retrieval system without the written permission of the author except in the case of brief quotations embodied in critical articles and reviews.

Revised and Updated Edition

Because of the dynamic nature of the Internet, any web addresses or links contained in this book may have changed since publication and may no longer be valid. The views expressed in this work are solely those of the author and do not necessarily reflect the views of the publisher, and the publisher hereby disclaims any responsibility for them.

All Scripture quotations, unless otherwise indicated, are taken from the Holy Bible, New International Version, NIV. Copyright 1973, 1978, 1984, 2011 by Biblica, Inc. Used by permission of Zondervan

"Come As You Are," written by Ben Glover, David Crowder, and Matt Maher, copyright © 2014 Thankyou Music

All rights reserved. Used by permission.

"Oceans (Where My Feet May Fail)" written by Joel Houston, Matt Crocker, and Salomon Ligthelm, copyright © 2013 Hillsong Music Publishing. All rights reserved. Used by permission.

To order additional copies or request reproduction rights please contact Small Revolution Publishing

info@smallrevolutionpublishing.com

Also by David Small

Small Stories
The Hope Project
The Wandering Leader
Nameless Faceless People

For Luke.
Thank you, brother.

Contents

10 Years...	xi
Introduction	xiii
Restoration	xv
Chapter 1	1
Chapter 2	5
Chapter 3	10
Chapter 4	14
Chapter 5	17
Chapter 6	20
Chapter 7	23
Chapter 8	26
Chapter 9	29
Chapter 10	33
Chapter 11	37
Chapter 12	42
Chapter 13	46
Chapter 14	50
Chapter 15	53
Interlude	57
Chapter 16	58
Life	63
Chapter 17	64
Chapter 18	67
Chapter 19	70
Chapter 20	74
Chapter 21	78
Chapter 22	83
Chapter 23	87
Chapter 24	90
Chapter 25	94
Chapter 26	97

Chapter 27	101
Chapter 28	105
Chapter 29	108
Chapter 30	112
Chapter 31	116
Chapter 32	119
Come As You Are by David Crowder	123
Epilogue	125
Acknowledgments	129
Want More?	131
Preview of Nameless Faceless People	133
About the Author	137

10 Years...

Ten years flies by. I can't believe it's been a decade since *The Wandering Beloved* was first published. Its been such an honor to receive feedback from people who have resonated with my story. I have received many deeply personal letters from people sharing their own struggle with depression, who have found encouragement in this book. I am so thankful for those who have read it and reached out to me.

As I am writing this updated foreword, I am sitting in a bamboo classroom while my team of students from the Jungle Discipleship School are performing a Christmas program for a bunch of happy kids. The kids have all fled from Loikaw and Demoso, Karenni State, and are now living in temporary shelters as IDPs.

A few days ago I sat in my hammock and re-read these words that I wrote in this book a decade ago. Some parts made me laugh and, if I'm honest, some parts made me yearn for the early days in my walk with God. Days when I would laugh at inside jokes with Jesus and was falling in love with the *real* God, not religion. As I looked back at this book, it was confirmation that a relationship with Jesus is not only available, but it's vital. No amount of rule following or church-going will substitute for entering a true and intimate relationship with the living Jesus. He is the same yesterday, today and forever, and we get to know him and experience him like Peter and John did. He is truly stunning.

The other thing I loved about revisiting this book a decade removed was being reminded that I don't need to make my faith complicated. It's a slow and subtle slide into "good deeds" and "Christian-ese" lingo, but sometimes we don't invite Jesus with us. Our relationship to Jesus can be simple and beautiful.

I remember feeling a bit terrified when I came back to Christianity that it would just be a fad. That, like previously in my youth, when my faith was to really get tested, it would prove fleeting. I was afraid to publish a book like this—which is making a pretty bold statement—and then a few years go by and it all peters outs. But what I've experienced is the exact opposite of that. God has constantly brought me into new frontiers in knowing him. Following God for the past decade has been the most incredible adventure of my life—and we're just getting started!

In this updated version of the book, I've attempted to leave the story and writing pretty much the same. I've adjusted some of the formatting and made some minor tweaks, but it's mostly the same story a decade later. If this is your first time reading *The Wandering Beloved*, thank you for entering my story, and the story God is telling. If you've read it before, I'd encourage you to revisit it and soak in some of the beautiful truths about our God.

The kids watching our Christmas program are howling with laughter as Joseph and Mary and their (comic relief) donkey make their way to the inn. It's the greatest honor of my life to be a part of the story God is telling here on earth. It's also a great honor to share some of that story with you.

David Small
December 2025,
Karenni State, Burma

Introduction

Wanna know what the problem is? It's God. Deep down inside, in that quiet place in our heart and soul, the problem is we don't know if he is real. I sure know that I questioned it. I once thought I was a young superstar in the church, a sought-after speaker for my generation, and a young man with a passion for God. But then I entered into the typical religious pattern:

I was hurt by the church.

I was betrayed by the ones that I looked up to as leaders.

I became bitter, and my pride told me that I didn't need the church anymore, so I walked away.

Then, I equated all of those feelings, all the hurt I had experienced, all the disappointment the church had caused me, with God.

It spilled over one night as I was out for coffee with some friends who were arguing about religion, and they looked at me with surprise when I blurted out, "How can I believe in God when I have a hard enough time believing in myself!" And I did. I was up to my eyeballs in stress trying to make it as a professional hockey player, trying to live out a dream that fewer than one percent of my fellow countrymen ever get to live out. How was I supposed to believe in a God I couldn't see, when I was having so

INTRODUCTION

much trouble believing in the guy looking back at me in the mirror? That statement, which is burned clear as day into my memory, was a turning point in my life. It was the point when I gave up on trying to have faith, when I gave up on God, and started to build a life centered around myself. My career. My wealth. My happiness. My empire.

And sadly for many people out there, my story is not unique. For many, being hurt by the church, embarrassed by "Christians," or disappointed in church leaders, is the norm. Then, we arrogantly say, "I don't need the church anymore"–leaving, not because we're angry at God, but because we've been offended by humans. Then, over time, our memory might fade as to the details or intensity of the pain we felt towards the church, and in its place is just a bitterness that we relate to God. We somehow, over the years of wandering, equate all the hurt, bitterness, disappointment, and anger with God. The institution and the leaders that represent it are no longer the face we feel angry towards; in its place is God. I did that. I took everything I was hurt about, angry about, and all the bad press that the "Christian" church gets, and equated all of those feelings towards God. And before we can ever enter into the final chapter in this *typical religious pattern*, we need to come face-to-face with that question that haunts us deep down in our souls. Is God really real? Is there really a God out there? And when he knows you're ready, he'll end a chapter of your life, turn the page, and begin a new chapter called Restoration. Once we know with certainty that God is real, then we can be restored into a relationship of love.

Restoration

Chapter One

"F@%! you, God! How could you let me feel this? You call yourself a God of love? Rather a God who allows suffering to happen. You think you're so powerful? You think you're so mighty, then show me, show me! Take off this blanket of sadness,"

I would shout at God. I would literally find a far-out, abandoned road through a farmer's field and then I would just have it out with God. Like David shouting his anger at God in the Psalms. I would hurl every curse word I knew at God, and I knew a lot. I would say things to God that would shock the most hardened soldier. How could a God of love and peace and justice give me an illness that was unjust, full of turmoil and hate?

I suffer from depression. God I hate this illness. I'm a runner, a soldier, and a hockey coach. On my last military training course, we would work for sixteen hours and then finally get dismissed for the day, exhausted and suffering from heat stroke, but I'd still go out running. Not for exercise, but in hopes I could run away from the pain my depression was causing. My course mates thought I was insane. They would see me streak past the windows of the mess, running full speed. I would run so hard and so fast, in hopes that the pain in my legs and lungs would outweigh the pain in my heart. It never happened. I would love the sweat pouring down my face - stinging my eyes, because then when tears would come out I could just blame it on the sweat. I would yell curse words at God. Gophers would pop their heads out of holes in the trail and see this maniac coming toward them yelling and running for his life and they'd disappear back underground to their peaceful caves. And that's what I was doing - running for my life. Running for sanity.

Depression is an illness that many people still don't understand, and for me it's the starting point of this book. Because to understand my story, I think it's important to understand depression. Depression is not just a matter of willing yourself to feel happy. It's not a matter of just "getting over it" or having a bad day. Depression is a physical illness. For me, depression comes in waves; maybe every five or six weeks I'll have a down wave. After a lot of blood tests and other tests from my doctor in 2008, I was diagnosed with a mild-to-moderate form of depression. The way the doctor explained it to me is that everyone's body produces serotonin, a hormone that helps regulate mood. My body doesn't produce the same amount of serotonin as a "normal" person's body. So sometimes when my body is low on serotonin, I feel like absolute crap. There are anti-depressant drugs called SSRIs or Selective Serotonin Reuptake Inhibitors out there. Basically they help make use of the amount of serotonin in your body already. They help balance out the feelings, and they help me feel normal. I don't take anti-depressants anymore: I found a better solution by creating my own multi-vitamin company. And when the better solution doesn't work, I just soldier on. In the words of one of my sergeants, "embrace the suck."

Depression is a physical illness. When I'm feeling beaten down because of my depression, I physically hurt. My heart feels like there are a thousand tiny needles poking into it. It feels like there is a dam of tears building behind my eyes for no reason. I could walk around the entire day feeling like at any moment I might start crying, even when it's blue skies and sunshine out. My energy disappears and I just want to lie in bed. My brain feels like it's in a fog. My muscles are sore. Many people think that dealing with depression is just feeling sad every so often. But it's sadness that comes on like a heavy blanket. Sadness that wraps itself completely around your body and weighs on you. It's a sadness that William P. Young describes in his book *The Shack* as, "The Great Sadness." It overwhelms and covers my life.

People have called me one of the happiest and most positive people they've met. People have commented how I'm always smiling and how I love to make others laugh and feel better. That's why it's always a shock for people when they hear that I suffer from an illness that is all about brokenness and sadness.

Brokenness.

It's a word that I've come to know too well. For me, depression is often felt most in the heart, where it's heavy, painful, and broken. So when people wanted me to accept Jesus, The Lord of Love, into my heart, I would just want to know if he could heal my broken heart. If he were going to come and live in my heart, would he fix my brokenness?

And when it didn't happen, I felt that I could hurl every insult and curse word at the heavens, that I could put the ball into his court. In hockey, when a player isn't performing, we call him out on it. We put the ball in his court, by harshly telling him he's falling short of expectations. He then has only two options on how to respond to the challenge: he can either step up and show us how great he is, or he can shut down. Either way it's a win for us as coaches.

If he steps up his game, then it's great for the team and great for the player. Job well done. If he shuts down, then we know he isn't for us and we trade him for something better, which will hopefully make the team better. I guess in many ways, I was doing the same to God. I was harshly, brutally, and honestly telling him that he was falling short of expectation and either he could show me how great he is, or he could do nothing - shut down - and I would know to continue on the path of looking for something new.

God is great.

Chapter Two

One of the first times I felt the guilt of religion was when I wrote a four-letter word on the chalkboard in the Sunday School room. I'm not sure why I did it. Maybe it was just that rebellious streak in me, but I remember it quite clearly. I was maybe seven or eight years old, and my mother was taking me to a church that met in the gym of an elementary school. The service would happen in the gym and the kids would be dismissed to the various classrooms of the small elementary school for Sunday School. And one day, I found myself alone in one of the classrooms and was struck by the feeling that I should be a "bad boy." So, I grabbed a piece of chalk, and in capital letters wrote the "F" word on the chalkboard. If I remember correctly it was in pink chalk. The next Sunday I was back at church with my mother and the minister said he was disappointed because the school had complained that someone was writing profanities on the chalkboard in the classrooms. The heavy weight of guilt fell upon me, and I remember feeling dirty. I had just figured out what it meant to sin.

I was raised in a pretty typical Christian home. My mother believed, and because we were her sons she would drag us to church on Sundays. When we switched churches from the church in the school to a Baptist church, she would bribe us with McDonald's if we behaved in church. So we'd go, and try to sit quietly and not start a fight with each other, in hopes that we'd get McDonald's on our way home. Wooden pews, dusty hymnals, and a minister who was as boring and dry as they come, for a boy who would rather be building tree forts or playing hockey, to sit for that long was pure torture.

My "religion" as a kid was hockey. It was the center of my universe, and it was everything that I focused on. I was playing for our city traveling team and loving every minute of it. When I accepted God into my heart, it was at Bird River Bible Camp, in a devotion session in the cabin with the counselors. I remember that it seemed like the right thing to do, and it made sense, and the counselor was super cool, so I prayed the prayer. I asked God to come and forgive my sins and to come and live in my heart and swore that I would give my life to him. I asked him to erase the four-letter word that I had written on the chalkboard. While I may not have fully understood what I was doing, I did mean it. I was sincere in my request and I really did want to believe in God and have him take care of me. But hockey season was coming, and whatever happened at summer camp would soon be replaced with road trips, swearing in the dressing room, and talking about girls.

Then we moved to Thailand.

When the idea was suggested that we move to Thailand, I was pretty much on board right away. I hesitated only because of hockey. They don't play much hockey in Thailand. But I remember clearly my friend Dave Treadway going on a mission trip with his family and how it had excited me to hear his stories.

I had gone on my first international trip when I was twelve years old. My aunt flew me (alone) from Winnipeg to Berlin, Germany, where she lived. I remember being alone in London Heathrow Airport and figuring out how to make it from one gate to the other. I remember days in Berlin when my aunt had meetings and I was left home alone. She told me not to leave the apartment; I was twelve years old, for Pete's sake. But, being the little rebel explorer I was, I disobeyed and ventured out.

I would first just walk a few hundred paces down her street, always making sure I knew where her door was. I'd look at the shops, cafes, bakeries, butchers. I'd listen to the people all talking in German; this new language sounded so strange but so exciting to me. I'd experience the new smells and sounds. Then I'd walk back to her front door and go upstairs so I knew I wasn't lost. Then I'd repeat, this time going farther away from the door. I'd go around the block, and then come back.

Then I found the subway.

I looked at the map, and I figured if I got on the train then I could go that way for a few stops, and then get on another train and come this way, and once I was back here I knew I could find the front door again. So I spent a few minutes learning how to buy a ticket, get the gate open, and get on a train. I'd go down one stop, get off, switch platforms, get on the train going back the opposite direction and then walk back to the door.

As long as I knew where the door was then I could go anywhere. If I could get from the baker to the door I could buy sweets. If I could find my way from the subway stop to the front door then I could ride the train. If I could get from one train stop back to her train stop then I could find the door. And as long as I was sitting like a good boy on the couch before she got home from her meetings, then I was fine. What a thrilling adventure for a twelve-year-old boy.

The next summer I was at Longbow Lake Bible Camp when my friend Dave, who lived on the opposite side of the lake, came waterskiing in. He was slalom skiing, and looking really cool. I hadn't seen him in a year because he had gone with his family on a mission trip to Venezuela. That night he shared with me all the amazing adventures he had had while he was in South America. I could almost smell the smells, hear the sounds, and feel the muggy heat. I had been in Berlin only for a few weeks, but that's all it had taken to be bitten by the travel bug. His stories of experiencing another country for an entire year seemed so cool. So when my parents asked what I thought about going to Thailand for two years, it was a no-brainer for me. I was sad to say good-bye to my teammates, but I knew that the stories and experience I'd have would make me a better person.

Then I got drunk.

It was the end of the world. Literally. The name of the music festival was The End of the World. I was working for the Ye Old Chip Truck, and we were setting up a food stand at the concert, which meant we would get free access to the festival grounds. So while I was there, I met up with a girlfriend, and her older sister kept sneaking us drinks, and before I knew it, I was wasted.

Somehow I managed to get a backstage pass, and mid-concert a rapper motioned to me standing in the wings that he wanted something to drink. So I stumbled out onto the stage, handed him a bottle of water, and then tripped over the wires falling flat on my face, in front of the whole town. That night I ended up in the tent of someone I didn't even know, and around three in the morning, stuck my head out the door of the tent and puked everywhere, right into my own shoes. The next day the headlining band, Great Big Sea, was playing their set, and I was feeling like it was the end of the world as I lay with a hangover in my father's car. This attitude of being a rebel, doing things I shouldn't, and living on the edge was one that I brought with me to Thailand.

God loves rebels.

While much of my journey to the cross can be chalked up to coincidence or just life happening, in the moments of quiet reflection it seems that God was preparing my heart. What if my aunt hadn't moved to Berlin to write music and hadn't invited me to visit? What if I had never experienced what it was like to explore and find my way back to the front door? What if Dave Treadway had never gone on a mission trip to Venezuela and told me all his cool stories? My heart wouldn't have been open and interested in his stories if I hadn't experienced Berlin. Maybe I would have made a big fuss about going to Thailand and asked to stay behind instead so I could play hockey; after all it was my Ontario Hockey League (OHL) draft year. Maybe in that quiet moment of "what-if-ing" the moments of my life, I wonder if God was just preparing me for a journey. He was showing me where his front door was so that I wouldn't get lost in the world.

It is a crazy world.

Chapter Three

There are moments that are stuck in my mind that I won't forget for as long as I live - moments that make for great stories around a campfire or barstool. For example, there was the night I got thrown in jail for being drunk. The day we drove deep into the jungle of Thailand to show villagers the Jesus film in their own language, and then prayed with those who wanted to become Christians. The nights spent in refugee camps along the Thailand-Burma border. The amazing feeling of smallness and peacefulness as I cross-country skied across Lapland. Driving a Harley through the Italian Dolomites. Skydiving over Verona. Sand-duning in the deserts outside Dubai. Nights of blackout drinking; of strippers, gambling, and relationships.

Relationships.

That word, for me, goes right along with the word "brokenness."

Since I was in grade two, when I stopped being homeschooled and started attending public school, I defined myself by my relationships. Early on, my friends were everything to me. I found my identity in my friends. I valued them to the moon and back.

Then, when depression started to become a big part of my life, it was my relationships that were the root of much of the pain. I would say things to my friends that would be hurtful. I would make them know I was angry with them or disappointed with them. I would shut down and withdraw only to see if they would pursue and ask if I was okay. Then when they didn't, it would make me feel even worse. When I would have dark days with depression I would expect that those friends I held so dearly would come running, full of compassion to try to understand and to help me. But people are people. They can only do so much. So when I would be sad, and they would be busy, it would just amplify the hurt. How can I then expect to have a *relationship* with God? It's the biggest area of my life I struggle with.

Isn't God ironic that way?

In Thailand God became real. My friends were all missionary kids who acted like good Christian kids, whereas in Canada my friends were all hockey players, who acted like hockey players. We had a great youth pastor who was genuinely interested in our growth and development. He was also interested in our hurts and doubts. He was the first Christian who I felt was real and not just doing a job.

I started to read my Bible, underlining verses, most of which had to do with friendship or relationship. Even at the young age of fourteen I was drawn to verses about love, joy, forgiveness, and friendship. I wanted to feel loved, because I was fighting an illness that made me feel worthless.

My relationships in Thailand were so important to me, and I felt that as long as we were all Christians, then we could spend unlimited amounts of time with each other. It wasn't bad to skip school to go to a conference worship service. It wasn't bad to skip out on family time or trips to spend time with our close Christian friends because we'd read the Bible and do study time and sing praise and worship songs.

I love to worship.

In Thailand I discovered real praise and worship music. Our church there was heavily influenced by Hillsong music from Australia, and I loved it. If there was one redeeming, deeply personal thing about my relationship with God, it was through worship times. I would ride my motorbike and sing praise and worship songs as loud as I could. I'd shout them into my helmet, sometimes even closing my eyes in praise. That isn't a good idea when driving motorbikes in Thailand. I'm a terrible singer, but I'd try to make a joyful noise regardless. During deep times of worship I would *feel* God. I would feel Love. I would feel peaceful.

Peaceful.

That was something I didn't know or experience often.

Last summer I sat with my friend Pastor Greg and explained to him, with tears in my eyes and agony in my voice, that I fight so hard for peacefulness. I will literally work as hard as I can to be peaceful. I'd stress so much about finding peacefulness. Being peaceful was a job for me. What an idiot. It was like peacefulness was something that would happen when I worked as hard as I could to find it. It was like trying to outrun the pain in my heart. If I just ran a bit harder, then I'd leave depression behind. If I just tried a bit harder, focused a bit more, was a bit harder on myself, then I'd find a way to have a peaceful heart. As the tears spilled over, I said to the pastor, "I haven't felt peaceful for over a decade. The last time I remember being peaceful was in worship."

When I think about Christianity, for me, it's all about relationship: with God, with Jesus, with fellow Christians. And as someone who is relationship-handicapped, that makes it hard. All of my relationships were so intense and so volatile. In my adult years I used the excuse of travel to not form relationships. I didn't really date anyone because I was always leaving.

Leaving.

A word I know too well. It seems for a lot of my life, my closest companion was the departures lounge in an airport. In Finland there was a girl I liked, but I never saw it going anywhere because I knew I was leaving in a matter of months. In Italy there was another girl, but my contract was coming to an end, and I knew I wouldn't be back, so what's the point? How can I have an honest, open friendship with Jesus if I'm constantly leaving my faith?

God doesn't leave.

Chapter Four

"God, I want you to work through my message today, work in the hearts of these young people, and give me your words."

I was going to be the next Billy Graham.

It started by accident, or so I thought, but I suddenly found myself preaching God's word. It took the full two years in Thailand to move hockey out of the center of my universe and move God into it. When I came back to Canada and got cut from the high school hockey team (first cut), I wasn't even upset. Instead, I decided to go work for God. I brought new ideas and energy into the church youth group; radical thoughts and concepts from Thailand, where our youth group had about 100 MKs who were so passionate. I started a morning prayer group at our high school. I invited people to youth events, and would drive all over town picking up and dropping people off so they could attend them. I would mentor the junior youth, and pray and praise with the senior youth, my peers. I was on fire. I'd cry with the youth through their struggles, I'd laugh with them, and I'd praise God when good things happened.

I went back and became a camp counselor at the place where I accepted God. I wanted to lead more people to Christ. In one of the final weeks, the chapel speaker had to pull out at the last minute and they asked me to fill in. What a awesome week we had: passionate talks, filled with the Holy Spirit, kids coming to Christ, and others bringing their worship to a new level. It was an amazing thing to be a part of. Then someone who had been a counselor at the camp asked if I'd speak at their church in Winnipeg, so I agreed. It was nothing less than exhilarating to be on a stage in front of a few hundred people and share a well-rehearsed, passionate message. I prayed ahead of time that God would use my message and give me the right words. But man, was it cool. Suddenly, I was this young rock star for Christ. I saw the youth pastor as a bit of a stick in the mud, so I took it as my job to make the youth group as passionate and exciting as possible. I was a wild stallion.

Then I met doubt.

More than a decade later I started to read the Bible. I didn't know how. Where do you start? So I was speaking with Pastor Greg and asked him. His advice was to start in the gospel of John, then read from there, in order, all the way to Revelation. He said you can read Revelation if you want, or come back to it later. Then go back and read Matthew, Mark, and Luke. So that's what I did. I started with the gospel of John, and although I knew the basic plot, and some of the main verses, something jumped out at me this time. The story of Christ, and the gospel of John is circled in doubt. No matter what Jesus would do, people doubted that he was really the Son of God. He'd make the blind see, he'd feed the masses, and people would still say, "You are not the Son of God, you are demon possessed." He'd be like, "Hey bud, what do you want me to do to make you believe! Walk on water, sure, no problem ... still doubting, here, I'll raise this dude from the dead, and then you've got to believe. Nope, still not. How about I surrender myself to death for you personally, and then rise from the dead three days later?"

Doubt.

This word slithered into my heart.

It happened slowly. How deep is my relationship? Do I hear God speaking to me? Where is all this going? Then I would preach another electrifying sermon, full of story and metaphors that would twist your emotions and pull your heartstrings in just the right way, so that when the call to action came at the end you were ready to jump from your seat. In looking back on my days doing altar calls, I don't hesitate to think that the commitments made, or the way God spoke to people through me, were genuine. But as I stood there preaching, I couldn't help but ask myself, how can I ask people to believe in something that I'm not even sure I believe in?

In my book *The Wandering Leader* I share one of my favorite ancient proverbs of the wise monk. A woman climbs to the top of the mountain with her young son to see the wise monk. She gets in front of him and says, "Wise monk, please tell my son to stop eating sugar." The wise monk looks at her and says, "Go away with your son, return in thirty days." So the woman goes away, and thirty days later she climbs back to the top of the mountain with her son and says, "Wise monk, please tell my son to stop eating sugar." So the wise monk looks at her son and says, "Stop eating sugar." Confused, the woman asked, "But wise monk, why did I have to go away for thirty days, why couldn't you have just said that a month ago!" and the wise monk responds, "Because thirty days ago I was still eating sugar."

I was asking people to come find God, to have a relationship, and I didn't know how to do that. I was asking people to have faith.

Faith.

Is it just me or is that the most difficult task that we humans are ever asked to perform? Acts of faith. How the heck does that work?

Begin *typical religious pattern*.

Chapter Five

It was the red baseball cap that was the tipping point. Man, did I make a lot of people angry wearing that hat in church. For me, my heart was totally in worshiping God that morning. But maybe somewhere deep down I was trying to make people mad.

I sat right near the front of the church. I closed my eyes and raised my hands during worship. And I did it all with a red baseball cap on. I could feel the angry stares burning holes into the back of me during the entire service. I barely made it out of the church that day without several angry and stern talking-to's. Those old guys who would grab you by the elbow, and, pretending to be somewhat joking to hide their rage, tell you how rude it was to have worn a hat into the house of God. Even the Christian men whom I respected either avoided talking to me, or came to rebuke me.

A few days later, the minister of that quaint Baptist church showed up at my house to discipline me. He had had so many complaints and protests from members of the church that he had no choice but to come and speak with me. I stood my ground. I told him God doesn't judge me based on how I dress; he judges the actions of my heart. I told him that the church is not a temple, but my body is the temple, and how my soul and spirit reaching out to God are Truth. The church is just a building that we can use to keep out of the rain and snow while we bring our brokenness to God. But church isn't about Truth, it's about politics, and the people have spoken, so the president has to act to keep his voters happy.

He lost my vote that day.

From there, despite the stopgaps that I tried to put in place, it wasn't long until I was done with it all. The last time I went into that Baptist church was for a youth Christmas dinner. Many of my old Christian friends were back from college for the holidays, and my brother and I wanted to go and say hi. We were down in the gym of the church talking with people when one of the many religious characters of the church came with one of their friendly elbow grabs and whispered in my ear, "We want to say grace and start eating, but we're not going to do it until you and your brother leave."

Roger. Message received.

Hurt by the organization. Check.

Hurt by the "religious ones." Check.

Equating all of this with "God." Check.

Doubt stronger than Faith? Check.

The moment that I had begun to feel doubt crawling into my heart, I put stopgaps into place. I figured if I could surround myself with close Christian friends who would pray for me, then I'd be okay. I threw away all my non-Christian CDs. I knew that if I was feeling down, I would turn to music. And if that music was praise and worship music, then my faith would be restored - that I would *feel* God again. That I would *feel* peacefulness again. I even taped up Bible verses around my room so I would be surrounded by Truth. I got baptized. I shared my testimony and was dunked under water. I remember thinking to myself, almost as if it were happening in slow motion, that once I get dipped into the water, and as soon as I come out of the water, that feeling of doubt that had nested in my heart would be gone. It was like being baptized was going to be the cure for the doubt disease. I remember clearly the minister putting his hands on my back and head, dunking me under the water, and then pulling me back up. I forced a smile, and he hugged me. The doubt crow hadn't flown away. It just sat where it had been perched before, watching this strange bath take place.

It's surprisingly hard to walk away from religion. It took many years for me to not feel guilt while sinning. When I was a good Christian boy and would sin, I'd feel the conviction of God. I'd tell myself to flee the devil and resist temptation, and I'd repent to God. But now that I was done with this whole God stuff, I didn't need to flee the devil. Temptation was no longer temptation; it was just living life. It's only a temptation if you're not allowed to do it.

Now that I wasn't a good Christian boy anymore, I didn't really know how I was supposed to live. I turned back to the only place I had ever felt welcomed, the hockey arena. It took some time, but eventually I let myself swear. Then after some years of growing as a non-Christian, I let myself drink and get drunk. I stopped feeling guilty when I would watch porn, and eventually even had sex. I learned how to play blackjack, and dropping a few hundred bucks on booze and cards at the casino wasn't a big deal.

Don't get me wrong; I wasn't a total train wreck. I held a good job. Mentoring young people and helping others achieve greatness was still important to me; it was just that the end state was different. Instead of creating champions for God, I was just creating champions for hockey. Instead of encouraging young men who were a part of the church, I encouraged young men to have values and skills. I got a degree; I still spoke, but now at universities and conferences on hockey and leadership. It took a few years, but eventually I settled comfortably into the world, focusing on believing in myself rather than on believing in something I couldn't see.

Commence Wandering.

Chapter Six

J.R.R. Tolkien said, "Not all who wander are lost," and I would have agreed with him for the decade that followed the red hat incident. From year to year I never really knew where I was headed, or what I'd be doing, but I never felt like I was lost. I knew that I had skills and strengths that would always allow me to be employable. I knew that I had a good heart, and that I enjoyed helping others. So, I did that. I climbed the coaching ladder in the hockey world. I got some scouting jobs with NHL clubs, I worked for Team Canada's junior program, and I coached clubs to league championships in Canada and Europe. I mentored young men, and I made some amazing friends in all corners of the world.

A decade slipped by rather quickly. And despite my rejection of God and religion, there was always one little prayer that I would say. In a short ten years, I successfully moved God away from the center of the universe, and replaced it with hockey again. I held some great positions, but also had some incredible lows. During that decade, I came to grips with my struggle with depression. The friends that I had were interested in drinking, partying, and hooking up with girls.

Welcome to the world.

It took me nearly two years to tell a single person that I was taking anti-depressants. It then took me another two years to finally stop taking anti-depressants. I wanted to be able to control my feelings on my own; I didn't want to rely on a chemical–and I didn't like the side effects of pharmaceuticals. I never felt that my drinking was a problem, but it definitely wasn't helping anything. Sunday night at home alone, drink a bottle of wine myself? Sure, why not?

While I maintained a fairly normal life by worldly standards, I did have some vices that would get me over and over. But my story isn't about an out-of-this-world turn from drugs and gangs like the story of Nicky Cruz in David Wilkerson's book *The Cross and the Switchblade*. Rather, it's a story about everyday pain. Every day, normal-person melancholy. The kind of confusion and angst toward the world that inspired Anne Lamott to ask in her book *Stitches*, "Where do we even begin in the presence of evil or catastrophe - dead or deeply lost children, a young wife's melanoma, polar bears floating out to sea on scraps of ice?" That's an image I can relate to: polar bears floating out to sea on scraps of ice as the general, normalized, everyday sadness we face. Just turn on any 24/7 news channel and you're sure to get your fill. How are we not all depressed?

But there was always that one little four-word prayer I would say from time to time: *Thy will be done*. Even as far as I turned away from God and the Bible, for some strange reason, I would just say this little prayer every so often. Maybe it was my excuse to think there is a *The Secret-* type magnetic power in the universe that will bring me what I need. Maybe it was just to release myself from having to worry about trusting my decision-making abilities ... that if I just made the decision and then said "thy will be done," then I could be even more disappointed in God when I made a bad decision. Or maybe it was just God, who hadn't turned an inch away from me, nudging me gently to submit.

"Thy will be done" is a great little prayer. It encompasses many things that I love about God. Simplicity. Faithfulness. A purpose for us that is good. When we pray "thy will be done," we're telling God that despite the fact that we're melting arctic ice and polar bears are floating out to sea, he's got it under control. We're releasing ourselves to a decision.

"Here I go, off wandering again." It was the result of a "thy will be done" decision. One that was bringing me to the airport, yet again, to fly off to Europe to take another coaching job. And as I said the words to myself, "off wandering again," I knew I had the title of my book. *The Wandering Leader*. I was a leader, and in leadership positions, but I was wandering all over the world. I was a wanderer. The word instantly took over all my marketing and persona. As my book was published, I began to be known as the Wandering Leader.

Then God said, "Oh Wanderer, come home."

Chapter Seven

I don't understand grace. Much like my thoughts on peacefulness, I have a hard time with grace. I feel like I need to earn it, yet God wants to just give me grace for free. For nothing. In a world where there are strings attached to everything, God wants us to have grace with no strings attached. Really. It doesn't make sense. When I screw up or hurt someone, I ask forgiveness, but then I feel like I need to prove myself worthy of his or her trust or friendship again. And I feel that when I sin, be it big or small, or a decade long, I feel like I need to prove myself trustworthy of grace. But that's not how it works. Grace is free for those who want it.

I didn't know I wanted it.

Heres where the story gets interesting. Unbeknownst to me, a few weeks before I ever met Luke, he was asked up to the front of his church so they could pray for him. Luke was heading off to basic military training, the first phase of becoming a soldier in the Canadian Armed Forces. His church minister brought him up on stage and prayed for his safety, for strength, and challenged him to be an example to others. To lead others to the cross.

The first time that I noticed Luke I was madly stuffing my face with food, hoping to get some calories "down range" before our sergeant forced us out of the mess to line back up for more marching and drill. There was Luke, bowing his head, closing his eyes, and saying grace. He wasn't trying to draw attention to himself, but he also wasn't hiding anything. He was just being himself, doing what he did. I envied the confidence. I made a mental note to befriend Luke and start to pick his brain. Over the next few weeks as we learned how to polish boots, clean rifles, and deal with chemical warfare drills, I explained to Luke how religion was stupid, how God couldn't be real, and how it was tough enough to believe in myself, much less something I couldn't see. Luke gave his point of view, he never tried to sell me into anything, he wasn't that person inviting you to coffee to get you to join a multi-level marketing company. He was just Luke. While I didn't really believe everything he did, we were still friends, and I think we both enjoyed the debates.

Seed planted.

Basic Training ended, we parted ways and communicated a couple of times over the winter. Nothing special. I wandered off to Italy to coach hockey; he went back to Edmonton to go to Bible college. As another hockey season finished with a weeklong binge-drinking session, I started to plan my military training for the coming summer. My next phase was my phase- three officer training. This is supposedly one of the more difficult courses that officers go through. Usually ten weeks of grinding down the weak and attempting to break the strong in Gagetown, New Brunswick. I'm not exactly getting any younger, so I wasn't sure how my body would hold up. I was also anticipating several bouts of sleep deprivation. For someone with depression, losing sleep is like pulling the pin on a grenade. It's just a matter of time before you explode. I was nervous.

I like the story of Jesus making the blind man see. Here's this dude who had been blind his whole life, and some random dude comes along, spits in the mud and then rubs it in his eyes. Personally, I'd be like, "Wow, back off buddy." But, when he wiped the mud from his eyes he could see again. This guy hadn't done much of anything except sit outside and beg for money. But he was given the gift of sight. He didn't deserve to see, and nothing was ever asked of him after this miracle was performed. He ran through the temple courts shouting for joy, proclaiming that Jesus was the Son of God. He just accepted grace. I wonder if a lone survivor of a tragic accident, or a student spared in a school shooting accepts grace the same way. I'm the guy who wants to work for things. I'm an officer in the Canadian Armed Forces; people are supposed to salute me and call me sir. Yes, it is a tradition thing, a legal thing, and a respect thing for the Queen, but I don't *expect* it from one of my soldiers unless I deserve it. In the same way, I suffer from depression, and it's hard to feel joy without having earned it. It's hard to accept that I can be joyful for no reason. My friend Dixie used to call them "content moments." She would say there are those moments where you look at your life and just feel content. I have felt these moments from time to time, but it's not easy. I feel like I need to earn joy, grace, and respect. I don't want people to give me charity; I want them to like the finished products in my business or writing or coaching.

God doesn't wait for the finished product; he likes us just the way we are. Right now. Today.

Chapter Eight

My clerk was sending me texts about flights to Gagetown. I was mentally and physically trying to prepare myself for this course. I was scared. I was coming off a short phase two training course where we had all been broken. We did things like wake up at two in the morning and run eighteen miles. No work up training, just go until your legs won't go any further. We marched through muddy fields, carrying heavy rucksacks, and were given sandbags to make it even harder. In eleven short days we managed to burn down an entire firing range, break two ankles, give a guy a heart attack, and fail forty percent of the course candidates. This phase two was the introduction to officer training, and I was heading into ten more weeks. I didn't know if I could do it.

Just minutes before my clerk booked the flight, he got an email saying I was switched off the Gagetown course, and instead I'd be heading onto the same course but in Edmonton, Alberta. Ok, who do I know who lives near Edmonton? Oh, Luke does. In fact, he lives ten minutes from the base. The night before I flew out to Edmonton, I sat in my room, head spinning from drinking a few bottles of wine at our mess dinner, and I said an honest, heartfelt prayer, the first one in many years. I later sent a text message to Luke and my friend Micha to share my prayer with them. Here is what my text said:

"I said a small prayer this evening: 'Lord, I don't really know where we stand, but I wanna commit these next ten weeks to you. I'd like strong knees, shoulders, ankles, and joints, but more so, if you're out there, I'd like your will to be done, and I'll just go with the flow.'"

I thought going with the flow would mean doing my best to keep up with push-ups and the ebbs and flows of typical military life. Little did I know I was jumping in slightly upstream from Niagara Falls, and going with the flow was going to send me on a wild ride.

Rainer was on my phase two training course with me. Purely as a mechanism of survival, I would sneak out of the armory when we were on our own time in the evening and go for a walk. Sometimes I'd just walk around the block and sometimes I'd walk to Dairy Queen and eat some ice cream. But I just needed to get out of the building that was the location of our suffering for fifteen hours a day. Even when we were so physically broken we could hardly walk, I'd go for a walk. On my second day, Rainer, whom I had never met before this course, asked if he could come along with me. So we walked. Sometimes we walked and talked. Sometimes we just walked and didn't say much. Then Rainer got put onto the phase three training course in Edmonton, and I was thrilled to have a friend who would be there with me. I was hoping we'd be able to sneak out on base for the occasional walk.

I come from the Canadian Shield. It's beautiful, with countless numbers of lakes, rivers, and acres of unexplored forest as far as you can imagine. I had lived for a year playing hockey on the prairies, and I had lived for a few years in the mountains, but for those who have never visited Edmonton, I suggest you add it to your list if you want to see some beauty. I've always loved the prairies. They are simple. The sky is amazing, so big. You can watch a thunderstorm approach from miles away. You can even see the rain falling long before it hits you. The sunsets last for hours, painting the sky and clouds with every shade of red, orange, and yellow you can imagine. There is peacefulness on the prairies. Farmers work hard; they fear God. They praise him when it rains, and curse him when it doesn't, or does too much. They are tough people. The kind of people who can drink whiskey without flinching, and sit on a wooden pew the next morning without fidgeting, or feeling overly guilty about their slight hangover. These cowboys are pretty cool.

My phase three course warrant decided that as long as we were pulling our weight on course, he would give us every weekend off. This is unheard of. But after week one, true to his word, he gave us our leave passes. I was looking forward to getting off base. Luke and I had been texting, and I had agreed to go with him to his church. I wasn't going because I was in the least bit interested in his church, I was going because I thought Luke was a nice guy, and that I would support him in his hobbies. He had a big family, and I thought it would be fun to meet them. Had Luke suggested we go for a picnic, strip club, casino, or church, it wouldn't have made any difference; it was just about getting off base and hanging out with my friend. But like the simple beauty of a prairie sunset, God has a way of getting us to look up and take our breath away.

Oh Wanderer come home.

Chapter Nine

The first Sunday was just a gentle nudge. It was a little tiny sign that would allow me to feel comfortable and not think that everyone in the church was a raving lunatic. This guy got up on stage and he talked about being debt-free. He talked about walking the Dave Ramsey baby steps, and how it was amazing to start his life over again without any debt. I like this stuff. I like Dave Ramsey. He's the best in the biz, a financial planner and bestselling author of *The Total Money Makeover*. For many years I myself had been working the Dave Ramsey baby steps and to be sitting in church, for the first time in a long, long time, and to hear this guy tell his debt-free story made me think the church wasn't so bad.

The next Sunday, Luke suggested I join him again. I agreed. God loaded his bullets and lined me up in the crosshairs. This Sunday, the minister got up and shared about his struggle with depression. He talked about how despite feelings of sadness and brokenness; the church still let him lead. This got my attention. It was like he was talking directly to me. He gave a very powerful message that day, and then the worship band got up on stage to play some songs. The first song they sang was called *Come As You Are* by David Crowder and the lyrics go:

So lay down your burdens, lay down your shame.
All who are broken, lift up your face.
Oh *wanderer* come home, you're not too far.

    Ugh. The lyrics were beamed onto a screen as the band played. My eyes snapped up from staring at my shoes. "Oh wanderer come home, you're not too far." That's my word! Wanderer. I was the Wandering Leader. "You can't bring my 'W' word here into church," I thought to myself. It's my worldly word, and this church place isn't for me. I've already given you the chance. Coincidence? I thought so. Then they played the next song called *At Your Feet* by Casting Crowns:

Here at your feet, I lay my past down.
My *wanderings*, all my mistakes down.
And I am free.

    Shut up. I could feel the tears welling up behind my eyes. Is it possible for the band to have picked two songs, back to back, that have my word in it? I wonder what the chances of that are. I'm not interested in miracles. I don't want your grace! My life is going fine without you. I'm learning how to survive.
    I got up and walked out of the service. Luke came out and said he could feel God moving, God calling me. I said I wasn't ready. I went and walked around the block until the church service ended.

God is a cool breeze on the marching soldier's face.

    The nice thing about the army, and CFB Edmonton in particular, is that you spend a lot of time marching around. The distance from our classroom to the mess hall was just over a kilometer, and we walked this several times a day. You have lots of quiet time when you are just trying to stay in step with everyone else and not say anything. You have time to think. About the beauty of the prairies, the big sky, and the way the grass in the fields dances with the breeze. You have lots of time for your scientific, logical brain to come to grips with coincidences. What are the chances of the worship band playing two songs, back to back, with the word *wandering* in them? What are the chances the preacher would speak about depression right before these songs were played? What was that feeling I was feeling? It was like something was tugging on my heart. Kind of like the way your heart skips a beat when you see someone you love, mixed with the excitement of a child waiting to open presents on Christmas morning.

Joy.

That's a word I don't know very well.

So after a week's worth of marching, here is what I decided was the result. I was tired. We get very little sleep in the army, and eventually that starts playing tricks with your brain and emotions. The message from the pastor was a nice message that I could relate to, and then the music had nice melodies and lyrics. These melodies and harmonies and lyrics about hope and rescue would make anyone feel tugging on his or her heart. It's no different than a nice country song. Music has that power to make you feel; that's why we love music. And the "W" word? Although I'm pretty sure the actual odds are pretty slim, it was no more than coincidence. It was a word that I recognize more than others, and just happened to pick up on it. Maybe I should have gone to buy a lottery ticket if I was winning with those odds.

Next Sunday comes. We get the weekend off again. Luke brings me to church. God rubs his hands together, "prepping grenade." Worship band starts up and plays a song by Amy Grant, *Thy Word*:

I will not forget your love for me,
And yet my heart forever is *wandering*.

I sat there shaking my head, staring at the lyrics on the screen in disbelief. Luke was just laughing.

Disbelief.

It's so easy to not believe.

My walking buddy Rainer and I had talked about my prior week's experience at church. At first I was hesitant about sharing it with him. I didn't want him to think I was going crazy. But when I shared my experience with him he said that religion fascinated him. This struck me as a surprise for some reason. He shared with me about Pascal's Wager, which I had never heard of. The idea is, if you believe in God and he does exist, then you're all good. If you believe in God and he doesn't exist, then you're still all good. You haven't had a bad life, and you haven't wasted anything. But if you don't believe in God and he does exist, then you're hooped. So the moral of the story was that it's better to just believe in God, whether you think he exists or not, because at the end of the day it's going to be better for you.

Go to work logical mind.

Chapter Ten

How to explain this week's wandering coincidence?

Left right left right.

This time there was no emotion in it. In fact, no offence Amy Grant, but the song is pretty old and not one I'd choose to listen to. There was no powerful moving message beforehand to soften my heart. It was just the song, the lyrics, and that word. Still, it can be just that I'm paying attention for it. Who knows, maybe this "wandering" word is used in thousands of church songs.

Coincidences.

There are times in my life when I have thought to myself, "Wow, what a coincidence," or "What are the chances of that!" In my first year of university I came back home for Christmas, from Finland, where I was studying. I ran into a friend in the liquor store one day. We hadn't seen each other for a number of years and had a nice time quickly catching up in the aisle. We wished each other Merry Christmas, and promised to grab a coffee before I returned to Europe. The coffee never happened. Life got in the way, I forgot, and then got on a plane back to Finland. A few weeks later I got an email saying that my friend was dead. Drug overdose. Heart exploded. This news was hard for me to take.

Years before, I had invited this friend to a church event that I had planned. That evening we had a great worship session and a woman shared a powerful message and then did an altar call. My friend went up and accepted Christ. It wasn't long though before he was back in his old habits: partying, drugs, and bad friends. He ended up in jail. I was his only friend who went to visit him. He wrote me letters as he bounced around jails across Canada, letters I still have.

My heart broke when I heard the news he was gone. I wept in my room in Finland. The darkness of the Scandinavian winter seeped into my bones. It was like a chill that wouldn't leave. Then, coincidences happen. I was at the Helsinki airport dropping someone off, and I saw a gang of English-speaking guys arrive, one with a tennis bag on his back. I commented to my friend, "Those guys will probably end up at my school." I was going to a sports school a few hours north of Helsinki at the time. After that comment I didn't think too much of it. I went back to school. A week later I was having dinner in the cafeteria, and I heard some people speaking English, so I went and sat with them. They were on a university exchange to run some sports clinics for three weeks. I started to show them around, and one of the guys, Tom, became a good friend. Although we were nearly strangers, we somehow felt comfortable talking with each other about things we normally wouldn't talk about with strangers; a lack of confidence, for example, or the loss of a friend. Three weeks went by and it came time for the boys from England to head home. I was sitting in their apartment helping them pack, when suddenly Tom came out of the room with a tennis bag on his back. Where had I seen that bag before? Suddenly I remembered that comment I had made at the airport. I asked what day and time they arrived, and it turned out to be the exact day and time I was standing in the airport. What are the chances of that? Tom has since become one of my best friends.

Coincidences.

Or, maybe God knew my heart was broken and sent me a

friend. Maybe God knew he could speak to me through worship music and put it on the heart of the worship director to choose certain songs. Maybe God knew that I was tired of wandering and ready for something more.

Week four at Luke's church. Bring it on. I bet we can't have a four-peat. Queue the music: *Come Thou Fount of Every Blessing* by Sufjan Stevens:

Prone to *wander*, Lord I feel it. Prone to leave the God I love.
Here's my heart, oh take and seal it. Seal it for the courts above.

Luke wasn't with me that week in church; he was away working at a camp. I texted him and asked, "How many songs does your church sing with this word in it? This is getting ridiculous!" Like a good friend, he responded by smacking me in the head: "More than I thought was possible! A good soldier should know when to ... surrender. Don't just wander around into a coaching job in Hungary, do actions that are intentional, that serve the purpose that you have been created for!"

I didn't reply.

Don't you just love those friends in your life that tell you exactly what you need to hear? Not what you want to hear, but what you need to hear. Having Luke give me a butt-kicking by saying the things I knew in my heart to be true was hard to handle.

That week at church Pastor Greg shared a message about being "all in" for Jesus. I knew the verse, either be hot or cold, but if you're lukewarm God will spit you out. I knew the verse well. It's like the wise monk who needed to stop eating sugar before he commanded others to stop eating sugar. It's like the army officer who should be able to do well everything he asks his soldiers to do. It's like the hockey coach who should be able to demonstrate skills for his players, rather than just expect them to be able to do them. It's like the young rock-star Christian who is speaking at churches and youth events who wants others to believe, but isn't sure if he does himself ...

I found Pastor Greg's contact information and I sent him a message. I shared with him how God had been messing with me and I told him that he asked us in the message that day to be all-in for Jesus.

I told him that I would be all *out* until I could figure out how to be all in.

Chapter Eleven

Just like when I turned away from the church, turning back to it takes time. These "blind can see" transformations don't happen in my life. Instead, it's like water boring through rock. Slowly, steadily wearing down. Smoothing. I was once told that when children see their parents living Christ every day, they will be more likely to believe in him. This struck me because my mom never stopped living Christ; even when her husband and all her children turned their backs on the church, she kept believing. She kept living Christ every day, even through the lonely days and angry days. I had been living my life on my terms for a lot of years up to this point. I was pretty comfortable in my routine. I swore like a sailor, I had a cell phone cover with a scantily clad girl on it, I chewed tobacco, and I didn't think twice about making dirty jokes. These habits don't just disappear overnight. And as I explained to Luke one night, I wasn't sure if I wanted to change.

Maybe it was the enjoyable talks I had with Rainer when I walked, or possibly all the marching we did with the army, but I had started to really enjoy going for walks. So when I'd stay over at Luke's place on weekends we'd often go for a walk. This particular night we walked way out across town. We sat on a swing set as I shared with him how I was struggling with all these questions. I don't want a religion that is based on emotions and nice melodies. Melodies fade, emotions change, and where does that leave me five months from now, or five years from now? I didn't know how to have faith. It's pretty easy if I just say, "Okay, a higher power is setting these songs up to send me a message." But even that fades. Even after a few weeks you can talk yourself into forgetting about it.

We sat on the swings as a huge prairie thunderstorm rolled in. It was around one in the morning, and we sat watching the lightning light up the sky. It was so beautiful, so powerful. The electricity from the sheet lightning could be felt in the air, making the hairs on your arms stand up. I shared with Luke that I have this cell phone case with a half-naked girl on it, and I didn't want to get rid of it. It was given to me as a joke by a couple players in Italy, but it made me think of them, and it made me smile. I wasn't ashamed of it. I explained to Luke that I enjoyed going out and drinking with my friends. I laughed a lot on those nights out. It was fun to get so drunk that you pass out. I didn't want to change. So how could I be all-in for Jesus if I didn't want to change? How could I have a Christianity where I pick and choose the parts I want to follow? All-in or all-out. Not half-in.

It makes me think of the apostle Peter. He was arguably Jesus' best friend, and was one of his closest disciples. He was with Jesus for three years, and despite the fact that he saw Jesus perform so many miracles, so many unexplainable wonders, he was still able to deny him. And not only deny him, but shout angry curses that he didn't even know him. How heartbreaking is that? That doubt is so deeply entrenched in our lives, that even when Jesus is saying, "Hey, look at this miracle," we'll watch in awe, and then doubt it ten minutes later.

The rain started to fall on us as the storm reached our swing set. I don't know for sure, but I could feel that Luke was praying for me as we started to walk back to his house. I told him about my struggle with depression and how I ran so much to make my legs hurt more than my heart. I told him that if I were to practice a religion, I'd want that religion to be all about Love and Joy. About happiness. I told him that every time I saw pictures of Jesus (hanging on the cross, holding a sheep, the Last Supper, etc.) he always looked so serious. I wanted a Jesus of laughter.

My friend Jay bugs me that I have three camera faces. Face one is the fake, awkward, terrible-looking forced smile. Face two is not paying attention, looking away from the camera, off in La La land. And face three, his personal favorite, is the head tilted back, mouth wide open, eyes closed, howling in laughter face. The deep, from-the-gut laughter. There are a few pictures floating around out there where I am just killing myself laughing, usually pictures with Jay. I want a Lord who is full of deep, howling laughter. How absolutely incredible would it be to just kill yourself laughing with Jesus? Imagine that! You're standing in heaven with Jesus, and he says something, the kind of something that is like those inside jokes you have with your closest friends, and then you just kill yourself laughing. You and Jesus are rolling on the ground holding your sides laughing. Jesus is holding his side as he laughs, his hand on a scar from where they pierced him on the cross. Why does it have to be so serious?

Relationship handicapped.

In order to have any sort of glimpse of having an inside joke with Jesus, it means friendship. It means relationship. Where do you even begin? My logical brain cannot understand God. I try to be a logical person. I have a science degree, and I like to be able to categorize things, or quantify things. I like things that can be added up, or put into neat logical sequences. But, try as I might, I can't quantify God.

When I left Italy in the spring of 2014, I was at the end of my contract with the club. Had they offered me a renewal I would have accepted it, but the board of directors was disbanding and no one could sign new contracts until a new board was formed. Deep down there was this feeling like maybe I should take a year off from coaching. But I looked for a new job nonetheless. An offer was on my plate to take a job in Hungary. It was a good job, and from what my agent was telling me, a good club to work for. They honored their contracts, paid on time, and were respected in European hockey. It was the exact position I was looking for. But, something didn't feel right. I didn't know what it was, but there was unrest about it. The club was waiting for my decision on their offer, and I told them I needed a week to think about it.

Left right left right.

March and think.

Pro's and con's.

Then one day, out of nowhere, the idea of hiking the famous Camino de Santiago in Spain came into my head. I had seen a movie about it many years before, *The Way*, and I had always thought it would be something I'd love to do, but it takes over a month to complete, and when would I have the time to do that?

The Camino de Santiago, also known as the Way of St. James, is an ancient pilgrimage from the south of France, over the Pyrenees mountains, and then all the way across Spain to the city of Santiago. It ends at St. James Cathedral, where you are supposed to get on your knees and shuffle to the foot of the cross. It's about 800 kilometers to hike the whole thing. I don't know why or where this idea of doing the Camino came from, but one day as I marched it popped into my head. But this didn't make sense. So I turn down this coaching job and go take a month to walk the Camino, then what?

The decision weighed on my heart all week. What would it mean to my coaching career if I didn't take a job? Would I lose the momentum in my career? Would I be able to find a job the following year? Am I ready to say goodbye to the hockey world? It was the center of my universe, and all I had known for the past decade. These aren't easy decisions to weigh. I was lying on the couch at Luke's place the following Saturday night, and before I drifted off to sleep I said a small prayer:

"*God, I still don't know where we stand, but could you give me a sign to help me make this decision about where I should go this winter?"*

Then sleep came. Then Sunday came, church time. I can just imagine God standing there with a grin on his face, nudging Jesus, saying, "Ready? This is going to be good, watch this." And in week five at church it wasn't the band that was the messenger, instead, a family got on stage to share about a mission trip they had just returned from. Where, of all places? Spain. Home of the Camino de Santiago.

I often think of the book of John and all those people who doubted what Jesus was doing. I don't blame them. It's not easy. I asked God to help me make a decision where I should go this winter - Hungary, or Spain. Then the very next morning a family is standing there talking about Spain. Of all places, too; it's not like Spain is a Third World country; in fact, it's a deeply religious country, with strong Catholic roots. Had there been a missionary family back from Thailand, or China, or Syria, it would have been easy to accept. But instead it was Spain. Jesus made the blind see, and they accused him of performing works of demons. What did they want him to do so they would believe? Hey, David, what do you want Jesus to do so you'll believe in him? What do you want him to do so you'll listen to him? He wants your heart. He wants you to know he loves you and has a plan for you.

Tears.

Chapter Twelve

"Hey, troops! Robin Williams is dead." We were sitting in a defensive position deep in the forest, in an exploded cigar formation, on a patrol base exercise. One of our staff was yelling this to us. Normally celebrity news doesn't interest me, but this news affected me more than I could logically explain to others. I grew up with Robin Williams. Not literally, but through *Patch Adams, Mrs. Doubtfire, Good Morning, Vietnam*. I used to train for marathons listening to Robin Williams' stand-up comedy on my iPod. I owned most of his movies and I loved his spirit. A man who loved to make others laugh.

Suicide.

The reason this affected me was because Robin Williams struggled with depression. And as talented, bright, and loveable as he was, if he couldn't handle the disease, then what chance did I have? I was angry at him. Instead of giving up and letting the disease take another life, he could have stood up and said, "I need help with this illness!" He could have helped shake off the stigma around the illness, and been an advocate for it. By bringing it into the light I'm sure he could have changed a lot of people's hearts and minds. Just by talking about it. But he didn't. I'm afraid.

THE WANDERING BELOVED

Today I feel like I've got things under control. Today I'm like the loveable Patch Adams, practicing excessive happiness. But, what if tomorrow, or next month, or in twenty years, like Robin Williams, I can't keep my head above the waves of sorrow? I wonder if Robin Williams believed in God.

I was starting to feel like I should look at the Bible. I couldn't logically explain all that was happening as I was attending this tiny little church in Gibbons, Alberta. I couldn't, in my right mind, chalk it all up to coincidence - ironically, my logical mind knew it wasn't quite right to do that. I downloaded a Bible app on my iPad. I didn't want other people to be able to see I was reading the Bible. The app had a study plan for depression that I decided to look at, and the first verse that jumped out at me was Romans 8:26:

> "In the same way, the Spirit helps us in our weakness. We do not know what we ought to pray for, but the Spirit himself intercedes for us through wordless groans."

This verse really touched my heart. I didn't know what to pray for; I didn't know how to trust God, talk to God, or believe in God, but I could possibly offer him a wordless groan. And he'd understand. The verse goes on to promise:

> "And he who searches our hearts knows the mind of the Spirit, because the Spirit intercedes for God's people in accordance with the will of God. And we know that in all things God works for the good of all those who love him, who have been called according to his purpose. For those God foreknew, he also predestined to be conformed to the image of his Son, that he might be the firstborn among many brothers and sisters. And those he predestined, he also called; those he called, he also justified; those he justified, he also glorified."
>
> — ROMANS 8:27-30

I want that. I want to give God my wordless groans, and that's enough for him to love me. This verse is a promise that my weakness is enough and that he has a plan for me. God picked me. He predestined me to be one of his children. Then he called me, through life lessons, through depression, through worship songs. Now he will justify me and glorify me. Why couldn't Robin Williams have held on to that in his heart? It would have made a difference. It has to.

So God was calling me. He obviously didn't want me to go to Hungary; instead he wanted me to go to Spain. God was trying to get my attention through my "wandering" word. A few Sundays came and went, and I thought God must be out of ammo. I thought, okay, there aren't any more church songs with my word in it. Maybe it could just be that the worship leader was at a point in his life where that word jumped out at him. I started to wonder if it was all just coincidence. Doubt began to take hold in my mind again. But, God wasn't out of ammo. The next Sunday, with the lyrics on the screen and the music playing, he opened fire again, reminding me he's still in control. *Oceans*, by Hillsong:

Spirit lead me where my trust is without borders, let me walk upon the waters, wherever you would call me.
Take me deeper than my feet could ever *wander*, and my faith will be made stronger, in the presence of my Saviour.

I realized that I'm not fighting a fair fight here. I can't explain this. It's too much. Then, suddenly, as I sat there, all these tiny little moments in my life seemed to make sense. Like they happened for a reason, to lead to this moment where I could drop to my knees and say, "God, I'm yours!" Before deploying out to Edmonton I got assigned a new fire-team partner named Micha with my home army unit for a couple of exercises. Micha was a great guy, great soldier, and had a great heart for God. He had been texting me throughout the summer, praying for me and encouraging me. I suddenly remembered the text message that I had sent to Luke and him so many weeks ago:

"Lord, I don't really know where we stand, but I wanna commit these next ten weeks to you. I'd like strong knees, shoulders, ankles, and joints, but more so, if you're out there, I'd like your will to be done, and I'll just go with the flow."

I should have asked for a strong heart, too. It became clear that, although my prayer was spoken from a place of fear, it came from my heart. I selfishly was just asking God to help me get through my military training. But I made that mistake of saying, "If you're out there, I'd like your will to be done."
Thy will be done.
His will was slightly different from mine. While I just wanted a healthy body to survive training, he wanted to show me back to the door. Like that twelve-year-old boy in Berlin, learning to get lost and find the door, I had been lost and God was showing me back to his front door. And he was standing behind the door, with a big smile and a huge hug waiting for me. Had it been God's will to move me from the Gagetown course to the Edmonton course? Had it been God's will to give us a good course so we could have every weekend off - something that is unheard of on this particular course? I suddenly remembered that a year prior, Luke's church had called him up on stage to pray for him and commission him to be a soldier for Jesus, to lead others to the cross.

I had yelled and sworn and cursed the heavens. Like the hockey coach that I am, I gave God an ultimatum: either step up your game, or get lost. Show me how great you can be, or I'm going to trade you for another player.
God is great.

Chapter Thirteen

I sat on Pastor Greg's back porch, tears in my eyes as he read the verse out:

"And you also were included in Christ when you heard the message of truth, the gospel of your salvation. When you believed, you were marked in him with a seal, the promised Holy Spirit, who is a deposit guaranteeing our inheritance until the redemption of those who are God's possession - to the praise of his glory."

— EPHESIANS 1:13-14

When you believed. Not *if* you believe now, but that moment. That second, when you say to yourself, "There is no other explanation." That moment when you're only nine or ten years old at Bible camp and you ask Jesus to come and live in your heart. That moment when you're a drug addict partier who comes to church and accepts God into his heart at the altar call. A deposit is made in you from God; he puts the Holy Spirit in you, in your heart, and says, "Here, I am leaving part of me in you, I am leaving my spirit in you, to guide you and help you hear me. I am leaving this to you so that you will know that you are guaranteed an inheritance." Not *if* you believe, *when* you believed.

God had never left me.

Isn't it ironic and beautiful that the one true place I had felt and experienced God as a teenager, through praise and worship, was how he would reach out to me as an adult? Through the lyrics to songs. Through writing and publishing a book, and placing that "W" word in me. Was it God who gave me the title for that book so that all of this could fall into place with his great plan? I had left him, and stopped listening to his voice. I had wandered all over the world, and gotten myself into all sorts of messy adventures. But God had never left me.

In Psalms 51:16-17 it says:

> "You do not delight in sacrifice, or I would bring it; you do not take pleasure in burnt offerings. My sacrifice, O God, is a broken spirit; a broken and contrite heart you, God, will not despise."

Thank God for that, because I honestly can't bring much more than a broken spirit.

Broken.

Micha sent me a song over the summer in Edmonton called "Keep Making Me," and the first line goes:

"Make me broken, so I can be healed."

Brokenness was something I could relate to. And it's perfect because that's all God wants. He wants our broken bits and pieces because then he can show you how amazing he is.

I shared my journey with my friend Brett. Brett was my captain a number of years prior on a team I was coaching, and one of my good friends. When Brett and I are together it's nonstop laughter. Brett has a heart for God. He was excited to hear my story and he wrote me back with an interesting image.

When I was doing all that speaking at churches and youth

events I would always use a story to paint an image in people's minds. I would begin the story, introducing them to the main characters, maybe a train conductor, maybe a father whose daughter has run away from home. I'd then leave the story and start to share the story of Christ and what he did for us. I'd explain what crucifixion meant, and then after I'd made them uncomfortable talking about the pain of death and the love to do it, I'd bring my characters back and finish the story. It was always a story of unconditional love and sacrifice. Of giving up self for others. And these emotional stories would be related to what Jesus did for us, then bam, altar call time.

I knew these stories well, but just like the story of Jesus, they were just stories to me. But when my friend Brett emailed me, he asked me to imagine that I had to die because of all the crappy things I had done in my life. All the sins I had committed, all the four-letter words I had written on chalkboards in Sunday School rooms, and all the times I had been a total disaster. He asked me to imagine that I had to pay for all these stupid things with a death sentence, but then at the last second before they took my life he said, "Dave, I got this for you, bud." That Brett took my place on death row. For some reason this brought tears to my eyes. I'd never let that happen. I'd never let Brett suffer for my stupid mistakes and decisions. Brett is my friend; I love him to death. Why would he do that? And just like that, it became real. It's what Jesus did. But the reason that the story of Jesus was only a story is because Jesus was never my friend. Jesus and I didn't have a nonstop laughing relationship like Brett and I did. He was just some dude who I heard about. He was the keeper of the rules, and the guy who made me feel guilty. I suddenly longed to have a relationship with Jesus that was like my friendship with Brett.

Relationship.

Ugh.

Imagine that Jesus was as good a friend as your best friend, as good a friend as Brett is. And then work your way through the story of Jesus' crucifixion. It would make me literally sick to my stomach to let Brett take my place for my screw-ups. I would bawl my eyes out, and have this feeling like I could never repay him. I would literally kick and scream and do anything possible to stop it from happening. I want a relationship, no, a friendship, with Jesus so that when I hear that he took my place on death row it makes me sick to my stomach. It brings tears to my eyes that my closest, dearest friend said, "Dave, I got this for you, bud."

As I thought about this an image of the cross came into my head. On the horizontal part of the cross was written, "I did this for you." On the long vertical part of the cross was written my name. David. The deeply personal God put in my heart the words; "I did this for you, David." He didn't do it for everyone. I wasn't just another number. He did it for me. Directly, personally, for me. He thought of me, he literally thought of every single sin I will commit in my life, thousands of years ago, and he said, "I'm doing this for you, David."

"I've got this, bud."

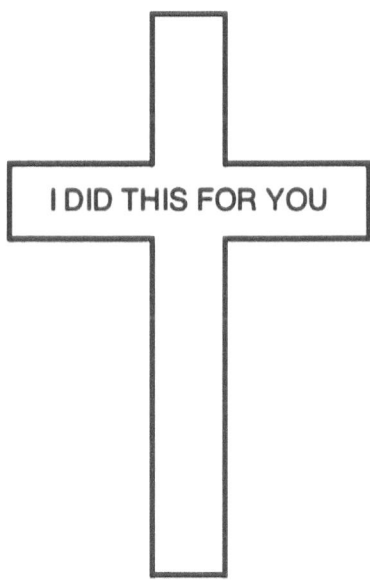

Chapter Fourteen

When I would walk with Rainer I'd usually put in some chewing tobacco and then we'd go for a walk. After all this God stuff, I still went for walks, and I still had the snus in my pocket, but I just never put it in. I don't think chewing tobacco is a sin, but suddenly I realized I had gone for two weeks without wanting to use it. I wasn't trying to quit; in fact, like I had explained to Luke, it was one of those things that I wasn't sure I wanted to quit. But, the urge was gone. Not by my will or choosing, that's for sure.

Then Jay came up to visit.

We had planned this for a number of weeks. We were going to get roaring drunk, laugh our asses off (or giggle our faces off, in his words), and then stumble home. We started at a Mexican restaurant, and after one drink I ordered water. He looked at me strangely, waiting for the joke to come. It never came. I thought I was going to have to fight hard to not give in to the temptation to party with my old friend. But it just wasn't there anymore. Literally, I had no desire to get drunk. I still wanted to have fun, and go out clubbing with him, but I would just do it sober.

It was this night that I realized that I was now different. I wasn't trying to be this holier-than-thou Christian; in fact, that was the last thing I wanted. I just had lost the urge to drink. I realized, though, that every single friend I had in my life, maybe with the exception of Luke and Micha back home, was a non-Christian. I have amazing friends, who love me, and will take care of me anytime I'm passing through. I've got great friends, with great big hearts, and I know they'd accept me no matter what, but suddenly I felt isolated.

I was talking with my uncle about becoming a Christian, and he said that it's like coming out gay. He told me this story about a friend of his from high school who, after many years, moved to my uncle's city and wanted to re- connect, but was afraid to contact my uncle. He was afraid because he knew my uncle was a Christian, and he thought he would judge him because he was gay. He finally got up the courage to call my uncle, they met for coffee, and he disclosed that he was gay. My uncle didn't care. But later my uncle was reflecting on the story and realized he felt the same way when he became a Christian and had to tell his parents. He imagined it being the exact same feeling, trying to have the guts to tell someone you're gay, or that you're a Christian. It takes a lot of courage, and trust that your friends and family will love you regardless. But it does change things.

After my army training ended and I came home, one of the first things I did was try to find my old Bible: the one I had befriended in Thailand, where I had stored photos, notes, and cards, and had underlined verses. When I found it deep down at the bottom of a dusty box in the crawl space, I held it, nervous of the emotions and feelings that might come by looking through it. One of the first papers that fell out as I opened the Bible was a bunch of quotes and thoughts I had scribbled down. Maybe from a sermon I was listening to, or just thoughts I was having, but I had written these notes, and the first one I read brought tears to my eyes, and then a later one made those tears spill over.

I was feeling alone; I felt like I was beginning to be a burden to Luke, but since he was my friend who had been there through this whole journey, I knew he understood. I texted with Micha a lot, and emailed a couple other old Christian friends, but in my day-to-day existence I was alone. So when I saw this scribbled note, crumpled in my Bible, it really hit home. The quote said, "If our questions leave us alone with Jesus, then lonely isn't a bad place to be."

It was comforting.

I was lonely.

It was as if I had written this note fifteen years before, crumpled it into my Bible and then said, "I'll need this later." If being lonely meant I could lean on Jesus, then maybe it was the best place to be.

God takes our broken moments, our lives, and our loneliness and uses it the most. Maybe he uses us broken folks more than others. I remember listening to praise and worship music in my headphones one night while I was lying in my bunk in the army. I was praying, and I started to pray for all my non-Christian friends. I loved them all so much, and I wanted nothing more than for them to be able to find God and walk this walk with me. I was listing them off to God and I said to him, "Man, there's so much work to be done down here." And then, clear as day, this thought was in my head like God had placed it there: "In *My* time, David. For now, let's work on your heart." Then, I was instantly made aware of a black spot in my life. I was instantly made aware of this spot in my life where I constantly gave in to sin, and all I could muster to say was, "God, I'm sorry, please forgive me. Make my heart pure." I repeated this over and over. All I wanted was to have a clean heart when I came before God. And as I repeated this prayer I felt this peaceful feeling fall over me, like a heavy warm blanket and just like before, the thought was in my head, placed there by God: "David, you're forgiven. I love you." The "I love you" wasn't a "comma, I love you," an afterthought tacked on to the end of the first sentence. It was its own complete sentence. Its own full, thorough, and complete sentence. "I love you."

I fell asleep.

Chapter Fifteen

I used to have a hard time sitting still in church. Why on earth would they make church pews out of hardwood? I want to go to a church with big comfy couches! I had an undiagnosed case of ADHD when I was a kid. I loved to run around, build things, break things, and fidget. Man, do I fidget. My leg bounces constantly, still to this day. It drives people nuts. I love it. Sometimes it was hard for me to sit through a long, boring sermon, and because of this hyperactivity in me, sometimes I find the thought of eternity daunting.

They used to tell me I could be with God for all eternity. For a lot of people, that sounded great. Like heaven. But for me, who often equated God with hardwood church pews and boring sermons, it didn't sound that great. I knew that heaven would be great and all, like there would be cool stuff to do, and maybe it would be fun hearing Job or Moses tell some stories around a campfire, but then what? What are we going to do tomorrow, let alone for the rest of eternity? I wondered if I could build tree forts in heaven.

When I returned home after the incredible summer, my life had been turned upside-down. I had turned down the coaching job in Hungary; who knew what that would do to my career? I had booked flights to Spain and was going to walk the Camino de Santiago. I had found God. Or maybe more accurately, he had machine-gun shot me through the heart repeatedly all summer long.

Again, you can call it coincidence, but Luke happened to be free and looking for something to do in the fall. He hadn't told anyone that he had decided he was taking a semester off school. We sat over beers one afternoon, and he listened as I told him my decision to walk the Camino de Santiago. I told him all about it, and somewhere deep down, I had this thought that it would be so amazing to walk the Camino with Luke, but it would mean he'd have to take time off school, spend a bunch of money to get there, and then come back in mid-October and find something to do. I decided to ask anyway. That's when Luke shared with me about his newly inherited free time he was going to have in the fall. He said he'd think and pray about it. The following week he texted me and said, "I guess I'm coming because all week I've been telling people I'm going to Spain." A month hiking across Spain with one of my best friends — it was going to be amazing. Then what?

Jay was planning to go teach English in Thailand and invited me along. I didn't want to teach English, but I thought maybe I could go back to this place where I grew deeper with God, and I could just relax, write a new book, and hang out for a few months. While I was pondering what to do in Thailand, I found myself in an argument in class about Burma. We were talking about insurgencies and counter- insurgencies, and we were asked to provide an example of when a counter-insurgency had been successful. One of the army candidates threw out "Burma," and I instantly started to get defensive.

You see, many years before when I was living in Thailand, I had gone to sleep in a Burmese refugee camp and I listened to them tell stories about rape, murder, and being tortured. I didn't realize, so many years later, that I still had a heart for the Burmese people. After I shouted down the other student's answer, I began to ask myself why I was getting so worked up about Burma. Then the thought to go back and help them came into my head. I was going to be in Thailand; maybe they could use me for a few months.

I did some research and found contact information for an old friend who was now the director of an organization working with the Burmese people. The organization had grown a lot since I had been there fifteen years earlier. When I was there, he was just a guy hiking medicine and supplies to people suffering on the frontline of the war in Burma. Now it was a real organization, with offices and people coming and going. I didn't think they would remember me, but I emailed the founder to see if I could come help. The next morning there was a response in my inbox: "David, we can use you as God sends you." Burma, here we come. When I got home and was looking through my old Bible, I found a quote I had written down that said, "I am ready for a Christianity that 'ruins' my life, that captures my heart and makes me uncomfortable." It's pretty easy to write that down when you're fifteen years old. Ruining your life at that age is not being able to hang with your friends, or having your PlayStation taken away. Being uncomfortable is just having to sit still long enough on those darn church pews. But fifteen years later, when I have a stable and growing career, a small business, blueprints for a house to build, and plans for the future, all this finding God business really does ruin your life. I went to church with Luke just to support him. Not for me. Not because I wanted something to happen in my life. Then, ten short weeks later, I can't deny it. I can't possibly in my right mind say that having all those songs line up for me isn't the work of God.

This Jesus fellow has gone and ruined my life. In ten short weeks I went from a comfortable and exciting life to a life turned on its head. I was heading out on the Camino and then off to Thailand, where I'd work with the Free Burma Rangers. My friends are slightly shocked and confused. I was thrilled.

The other day I was thinking about eternity with Jesus. I still don't know how to understand what I'm going to do for an eternity. I still bounce my leg and can't sit still for a long time. But when I was thinking about eternity, maybe I don't really know what that means, but if I could start by spending ten thousand years just looking Jesus in the eye, that would be a good start.

Interlude

Chapter Sixteen

Over the summer God grabbed my attention through the lyrics to songs. Repeatedly, some form of the word *wander* would show up in the weekly grouping of songs. At the beginning, I would just mark it up to coincidence. That's the easiest way to do it when you aren't sure if there is really a God out there. But, the thing about your logical brain is that as much as it works to figure out how coincidences works, it must work equally as hard to figure out if it's too much to be a coincidence.

When I returned home I decided that to put my logical brain to rest, I needed to figure out the chances that I could hear that specific lyric each week, over and over, during the summer. What will follow is my search for that exact answer, and I will warn you, dear reader, that the following is going to be a bit of math and technical talk. You're welcomed to skim through this brief interlude, or skip into the next chapter, but I'd encourage you to bear with me as I explain this to you.

To begin with, I started to do research on church songs that are sung in church these days. I began to compile lists. I would search for the top 100 hymns of all time, top church songs sung today, top praise and worship songs of all times, Billboard Christian charts going back the past ten years, and on and on. Eventually I had about a dozen lists, and then went through and cross-referenced all the lists, deleting all the duplicates. I ended up with a list of just over 500 songs. From that list, I went through and searched for the lyrics of every single song. This process took the better part of a week to do. I looked for any form of the "W" word: wander, wanderer, wandering. After going through all of the songs, I found ten out of 500 songs that contained that word.

So then I put the question to one of my friends who is a mathematician. Sean works for Finance Canada and his brain works on a totally different level than mine (or most people's, for that matter.) I gave Sean the following question:

A man listens to the radio every Sunday for eight weeks. He listens to only eight songs each Sunday, and then turns off the radio. The DJ who plays the songs has a library of 500 songs to choose from. The DJ will never repeat a song once he has played it once. (For example, if the DJ plays Song 23 on week 1, Song 23 will never be played again for the remaining seven weeks.) The man listens to the songs for one specific word/lyric. That particular lyric appears in ten of the 500 songs. What is the probability that the man will a) hear a song every week for eight weeks that has that special lyric in it, and b) what are the chances that the man will hear two songs, back to back, in the same week, with that special lyric?

So let's clarify a few things. The man is me, the radio is church; I went eight consecutive weeks and had a moment with God each of those weeks. While my list of 500 songs is not exactly exhaustive, obviously there are more than 500 songs that could be sung in a church; I feel that it's a pretty accurate list. As I started to go through the lyrics of the songs, the "W" word would appear in approximately two percent of the songs; this percentage stayed fairly consistent as I moved through all 500 songs. From this, I can assume that if there were 500 or 5000 songs, it would remain approximately two percent that would contain that lyric. I assumed that the church would play approximately eight songs per weekly service. I assumed high just to give myself the worst possible odds; I think the average service was more like five or six songs, but for argument's sake, I assumed eight songs. The DJ in the question represents the worship leader at the church. A song was never repeated while I was there.

My friend took the question and a few days later came back to me with an answer. I am by no means any good at math, so most of what he said was Chinese to me. If you're any good at math, then you may understand some of this. Since I can't exactly paraphrase his words, I'm just going to copy and paste part of his email response to me exactly as he wrote it:

The odds of hearing it once in Week 1 are the number of ways you can pick a song with the lyric; 10 (since 10 songs have it) x the number of ways you can pick 7 songs without the lyric (490 choose 7, since 490 songs don't have it and you need 7 of them). Then that must be divided by the number of ways to choose 8 songs from 500.

So the product of those gives the probability of hearing it exactly once each week and the probability is about 1/150,000,000.

Computing the probability of hearing it twice in a week and once the rest of the weeks is similar, assume hear it twice Week 1 and then use conditional probability of hearing in Week 2 given heard 2x in Week 1. Then multiply this probability by 8 since week where hear it twice could be any week and they are all equally probability. Similar procedure for three times in a week. Similar for twice in two weeks, but you assume hear it twice in Weeks 1 and 2 and then multiply by 8choose2 since it could be any two of the eight weeks.

Final answer is 1 in 112,000,000. I ran a few thousand simulations in Excel and it never happened.

Wow.

So, allowing for a few slight assumptions (e.g. my list only had 500 songs, but I assumed a two percent occurrence of the special lyric) we end up with a 1 in 112 million chance of having the lyric randomly picked and show up every week for eight weeks. Imagine how the odds would change if they only sang five or six songs in church each week? Now, I ask you the question: if this lyric showed up randomly every time I stepped into that church, is it just that I was paying attention for the word and it was just a coincidence? What percentage can we consider a miracle?

Today it brings me some comfort to know that God's love for me is that powerful. God didn't show me 50/50 odds. If I was really not paying attention or awake, I could have missed it one or two Sundays in a row, but to have that much repetitively poured out on me is really incredible. Makes you feel pretty special when the Creator of the universe tells you that you're 1 in 112 million.

Ok God, you're real.

Now what?

Life

Chapter Seventeen

Have you ever been in a church service or place where you can *feel* God? I remember a couple times when I was younger, thinking I could really feel God's presence. It was like some energy was moving through the building. Everyone felt a stirring in his or her heart. Think of a revival, or a really powerful message that speaks to your heart, or a passionate worship service, maybe the last minutes with a dying relative. And that's just God *whispering* to us–imagine actually standing before him.

At one point I thought I had "beat" depression. I was seeing a really good counselor in London, England. I had weaned myself completely off of the anti-depressants. I had rebuilt my confidence and my career. I was at a good spot in my life. Then it all came crashing down. A few short months later and I found myself at one of the darkest points in my life. I didn't want to leave my bed. Curtains drawn, I would surround myself in darkness and just sleep. For weeks. I had to keep telling myself to be like Tom Hanks in *Sleepless in Seattle*, "I'm gonna get out of bed every morning ... breathe in and out all day long. Then after a while I won't have to remind myself to get out of bed every morning and breathe in and out ..." It was either that or kill myself.

I remember at this point trying to practice one exercise that my counselor had given me. He had asked me to write down ten positive things about myself. Ten good qualities or characteristics about myself. The idea behind this exercise is to write down your list of ten, then ask yourself, "Would you want to be friends with (or date/marry/be led by) a person who was ..." and then read through your list. Do you know how hard this is to do on a good day, let alone when you're feeling down? I remember sitting there, racking my brain, and couldn't come up with more than one or two things. Try this right now. Write down, in the margin, ten things about yourself that you like or that are good qualities. Here's my ten today: generous, friendly, funny, honest, genuine, open, intelligent, experienced, well traveled, and worshipper.

I remember so clearly thinking about how it was so hard to come up with even ten things about myself that I liked. One or two came pretty easy, but then I really had to work to find the rest. It was kind of sad. That's why it was a real shock to me when I found out that Jesus not only loved me, but he also liked me.

Jesus loves me, this I know, for the Bible tells me so.

We all know the song; we grew up singing it in Sunday School. Yes, Jesus loves me. That's cool. But the thing that moved me more was when I realized that Jesus liked me. For real. I think there is a difference between loving someone and liking someone. When I was growing up, my brothers and I always loved each other - we didn't always like each other though. Some days we would rather beat the tar out of each other. But we always loved each other.

Jesus likes me, though, all the time. He could write a list a mile long of all the qualities about me that he likes. He wouldn't even need to think twice about it. While I beat my brains out trying to come up with just ten things I like about myself, Jesus has this huge list ready.

We can be so hard on ourselves sometimes.

We've got the most powerful being in the world. So powerful that when he just quietly whispers to us in that deep place, we can feel the whole room be energized. Just a soft, gentle whisper is enough to knock us on our knees. With a roll of the eyes and a quick rebuke, Jesus can calm raging storms. He's so powerful. Then he can turn around and tell you every single thing he likes about you without any hesitation. Why can't we just surrender to that sometimes? We've spoken these lies and half-truths to ourselves for so long that we have a hard time listening to Truth. We beat ourselves down so much before we even leave the front door of our house.

I used to love going for walks in Edmonton. The sky is so amazing in the prairies. Every night it was different, and every night it would have the ability to take your breath away if you let it. Some people don't even bother to look up. But if you look up, and let yourself say, "Wow, that's beautiful," then the sky will take your breath away. The prairie sky is one reason I recommend that everyone should visit Edmonton one day.

I'm so happy to be friends with a Jesus who is like the prairie sky—strong, colorful, bold, big, powerful. And when I give myself permission to look up, I sometimes can't help but have my breath taken away.

After restoration, comes life.

Chapter Eighteen

Depression is the love of your life breaking up with you every fifteen minutes for a whole day. It's a jackhammer to the heart. It's waves of pain, sadness, and sorrow crashing on you over and over and over, and you're lucky if you remember to breathe between each wave. It's being totally exhausted but not being able to sleep. It's a contraction of the heart; it's Satan's laughter. It's lonely.

"I'll pray for you."

It's that thing people say when someone bears a broken heart or life before them and they don't know how to respond. "I'll pray for you." When I was going through wave after wave of suffering, and I shared with my friend, he said, "I'll pray for you." And my first thought was, "I don't want you to pray for me, I just want you to be my friend!"

In my head, I had this picture of a beautiful sunny day at the beach. Blue skies, sunshine, birds flying, everyone enjoying the day. Then there was me out in the waves, in the gully between two waves where you have a minute to take a breath before the next wave crests and crashes right onto you, pummeling you into the ground; you roll, turn, drag, and scrape along the bottom of the ocean, your lungs filling with water.

That wave was called Sorrow.

As you recover, trying to find your footing and remembering to breathe, you get a glimpse out to sea and you can see large rolling waves coming for as far as the eye can see. Each wave has a name: Pain, Grief, Longing, Hurt, Loneliness, Shame, Embarrassment, Brokenness. They just continue as far as you can see, out past the horizon, all coming to crash on you. I don't want you to pray for me, I want you to swim out and play in the waves with me. For you the waves don't have any names, they're just fun to ride and play in. For me, they're torture, but if you're just there with me, it helps. I think about Bob Goff and his book *Love Does;* Love does stuff, it's an action word, not a feeling or emotion. I don't want your prayers; I want your friendship.

I know that God is all-powerful and that prayer is one of the greatest things you can give someone, but sometimes it just feels like a cop-out. I remember hearing a speaker say that if everyone *actually* prayed for all the people that they said they were praying for, life would be really different. I will pray for my friends, every day before bed, I'll spend time praying for the people I love, and sometimes the people I don't love, but I also want to be love in action. Jesus was. Jesus was love walking in a pair of sandals talking to people who needed love. He wasn't afraid to hang with some real losers of the world; prostitutes, thieves, the worst of the worst illnesses, and he didn't mind showing up at a few wild parties. I think sometimes when I spend time in prayer, it helps me work through certain thoughts, and it also brings people to my mind or onto my heart to pray for, but then it's about taking action too. I'll lift you up in prayer, God will listen to the prayers, and then I'll do what I can to be Love.

Depression is real. You can't point to it, put a cast on it, or see it on an x-ray, but it's real. You just need to trust me when I tell you I'm hurting. You just need to have faith that the things I'm telling you are true. God is real too. You can't see him, you can't trap him or use a special machine to find him, but he's real. You just need to trust him when he calls you. You just need to have faith that the things I'm telling you are true. I struggled with faith long before I even knew what depression was. Then, for years, I struggled with my feelings, not believing depression was real. Thinking I could outsmart my feelings, or sleep it off, or use my logical brain to tell myself what truth is. It didn't work. No matter how much I tried, no matter how much I slept, I couldn't beat depression. Finally I started to look for help and answers. I went to our team doctors, I did blood tests, I learned about the history and facts about the illness. Then the pieces of the puzzle started to come together, and the more I learned, the more I believed. I still couldn't see depression, but I knew that it was what I was experiencing. It's real.

It's funny to me that God would give me this illness in my life because I think he knew that it would help me in my struggle with faith. There were times when I was asked to preach about Jesus at churches or youth meetings, but deep down inside I didn't know if I really believed it. I tried all I could to believe, I listened to Christian music, I prayed, I went to church and even sometimes listened when the preacher was preaching. But it didn't work. My doubt won, and I left it all behind for a decade. God was preparing my heart.

As I learned about depression, I learned how to have faith in something I can't see. I need to trust that when I feel like waves are crashing over me, it's real pain. I also need to trust that when I feel God calling me, pursuing me, and telling me he'll play in the waves with me, it's real Love. Jesus never told anyone who came broken before him that he'd pray for them, and then just walked off and forgot. Instead, he jumped in and played in the waves with them until the storm died down. Sometimes, he even calmed the storm himself when he knew we might not be able to keep our heads above water.

Love does stuff.

Chapter Nineteen

When I walked across Spain on the Camino de Santiago, I came across a lot of Catholic churches, and attended a few Catholic masses. This was my first introduction to mass. The humanity that makes the gospel of Jesus so amazing seemed lost to me in Catholic traditions in Spain. There were these terribly awkward pictures of baby Jesus, sitting on mother Mary's lap. He's wearing a crown and fine robes; he's holding up two fingers as if to bless all the people. This baby never had a poopy diaper, he is super baby.

> "For this reason he had to be made like them, fully human in every way."
>
> — HEBREWS 2:17A

Jesus was fully human.

This took me a long time to get my head around, but before I could fully appreciate his divinity, I had to learn to appreciate his humanity. Jesus had to learn how to tie his shoes (sandals?), he had to be potty trained, I'm sure there were nights that he would cry into the night, keeping Mary and Joseph awake. I wonder if

THE WANDERING BELOVED

they ever rolled their eyes and said, "Are you sure this baby is from God?" Jesus wasn't super baby like they make him out to be in Spain, he was a human baby, he had to learn how to speak, he had to be taught the colors, what an apple was, and how to build things. I'm sure he fell and scraped his knees, stubbed his toes, and cut his finger helping Joseph do carpentry work.

I left CFB Edmonton after my summer experiences with God and I returned home. I was on this mountaintop high of being restored, rather miraculously, to God. But as it turns out, it's much harder to live your faith when you leave your safety bubble. I had been surrounded by army routine, and then church on the weekends. Life was easy. Once I left the army, I had to face my family, my friends, and old places of pain. I didn't know how to live as a Christian. I was talking with Luke about it one night and he quoted a verse that says, "I am not ashamed of the gospel" (Romans 1:16). I began to think about this verse, and asked myself, honestly, am I ashamed of God? Am I ashamed of Jesus, or to say that I follow the teachings of the Bible? It takes a lot of time and honesty to think about the answers to these questions. What I came up with surprised me.

I'm not ashamed of the gospel. I'm not ashamed of God; I believe he called me out—how can I explain it any other way? The most powerful being in the universe, the one who created the universe, pursued me. Me. Specifically me. I am not ashamed of that; in fact, I'm so honored and proud. I am not ashamed of Jesus. As I embrace his humanity, his embodiment of my sinful nature, and his character, I can't help but love this teacher. So what was my problem with living out Christianity proudly?

I was ashamed of Christians.

In Spain it became really clear why. The Catholic Church is like a club for depressed people. The priest mumbles something, sometimes in Latin, into the microphone, and the congregation mumbles something back to him. There is no thought in it, no heart in it, no joy in it. It doesn't seem to be about relationship; it's about rules and traditions. We wanted to go up and take communion during one mass, but we weren't allowed, because we weren't in the "Catholic club." The cathedrals are huge, massive fortresses with gold altars at the front. I don't want to be part of this club. All throughout the cathedrals are crosses and pictures of Jesus hanging on the cross dying. Every single picture of Jesus I saw in Spain shows a man who looks like he's carrying the weight of the world on his shoulders. Jesus was a man of joy and laughter. He was fully human, he got tired, he got hungry, he wept, he got angry, he needed time on his own to recharge the batteries, he laughed, he made jokes and he was playful. He wasn't Superman. He was man.

Christians are painted in broad strokes, and usually not "because of their love," but all too often because of their stupidity. I read about Christians going to protest at a funeral for a kid who was beaten to death because he was gay? Mom and Dad are weeping next to the coffin, and there in the background are a bunch of Christians holding signs saying, "Adam and Eve, not Adam and Steve!" Or how about Christians years ago holding up the Bible towards their slaves and saying, "The Bible says slaves should obey their masters." How about Christian priests and their altar-boy fetishes, or abuses suffered under Christian armies?

Painted with broad strokes.

As a hockey coach, I came to the realization early on that I could get more from my players if I got to know each of them as people. The one-size-fits-all style of coaching doesn't work anymore. That's old school. I've come to realize that my players are all different people who are motivated by different things. One player might be motivated by technical talk, another by putting my arm around him and showing him some love, and another by yelling and telling him to wake up. I wonder if pastors of churches should approach their congregations in the same way - getting to know them personally, getting to know what draws them to the church, and then using that to motivate them to go deeper into their relationships with Christ.

I'm drawn to joy. I'm drawn to peacefulness. I'm drawn to

love. Stories of end days, and pictures of Jesus looking manic depressive don't do anything for me. I've got enough of that in my life; I don't need to be reminded of it every time I see Jesus.

I'm ashamed of Christians who totally misrepresent the character and heart of Jesus.

Chapter Twenty

I don't understand how people can believe in God, but not in Jesus. Or believe in spirits, but not in God. I don't understand how people can believe in ghosts, satan, or hell, but not in angels, God, or heaven. It seems a bit strange.

I began to read my Bible, in the order that Pastor Greg told me to, starting with the gospel of John, then through to the end of the New Testament, and then back and read Matthew, Mark, and Luke. It's not an easy book to read. It was fairly easy in the book of John; it's just the story of Jesus' life. And then stories about the apostle Paul were not bad; he's a bit of a badass, so I could relate to him in some way. But then after that things get so confusing. Characters have different names for the same person, then there are the many Johns, whom I can never keep track of which one is which, I realized I couldn't name all twelve of Jesus' buddies, and half the time things are written in tongue-twisters and parables that I don't get. At first when I was trying to read the Bible I was reading it like I'd read a James Patterson book. I would pick it up off my bedside table and I'd read it before bed. I'd judge it, just like I'd judge Patterson's newest Alex Cross story. In my mind I'd be saying things like, "This isn't very good writing," or "This plot is a bit weak," or "This wording would make my editor go crazy." I was just forcing myself through it.

Then I saw Luke's Bible.

Luke has sections of his Bible that are underlined nearly every part of the page. I had just finished reading the book of Romans, and hadn't underlined or highlighted anything. Then I looked at Luke's Bible, and almost the whole book of Romans was underlined. I felt like an idiot. Did I miss something?

I enjoyed reading the gospels and the story of Jesus. I love the character of Jesus. And around the same time I was reading a book called *Beautiful Outlaw* by John Eldredge. I think all new Christians should read this book and walk 800 km along the Camino de Santiago with a trusted Christian friend, or the one who introduced them to Christ. I think we'd see a different Christianity. As I was reading the Gospels, and learning about the story of Jesus, I began to wonder, if I were alive in Jesus' day, would he have picked me to be one to follow him? Would I have been one of his twelve disciples? I wonder how my story would have read in the Bible. Would my heart, as it is today, be soft enough to hear Jesus' message? To believe? I want to believe I would have been like Simon Peter. I would have had trouble believing at times, I would have been as stubborn as an ox, and I would have been over-the-top in love with Jesus. At least I hope so.

I love the story where Jesus appears to the boys out fishing after his resurrection, and when Simon Peter realizes it's Jesus on the shore, he jumps out of the boat and thrashes his way to shore. I love it. He's the guy who asks the question all the other disciples are thinking but too afraid to ask. He's the one who just blurts stuff out without fully thinking. He's the one who, I'm sure, made Jesus laugh at times.

As I began to reintegrate into my old life, away from my support network, I came crashing down. I was trying to read the Bible, but it just seemed like most of it was so confusing. I was trying to live the right way, but old habits and temptations have a strong hold that is hard to break. I suddenly found myself sinking.

I think of Simon Peter, in John 21, when Jesus has been resurrected but disappeared, Simon does what he knows—he goes fishing. He spent three years with Jesus, he saw him rise from the dead, and then within a matter of a few hours of not knowing where Jesus has gone off to, he decides to go back to his old life. He goes out fishing.

I came crashing down off the mountaintop with the force of an avalanche. How do I live out this new faith and belief? I don't know how to do this. I felt awkward and strange talking to people about what happened over the summer, even my mother, who was overjoyed that I had experienced God. It just felt weird. I had experienced this amazing mountaintop experience in the summer, being called back to God, and then I came crashing down. It seemed that within a few hours of leaving Edmonton, I went back to my old life and old way of living.

When I was out walking the Camino, there were a few tough days in the mountains. My knees were still pretty busted up from my army training, and I realized that it was much more painful to come down the mountains than to go up them. Hiking up the mountain takes your breath away; the higher you go the more amazing the views become. But going down is painful. I realized my faith was the same way. I had some amazing views of God from the mountaintop of the summer, but then I came crashing down, and it was painful. I needed to learn how to come down off the mountaintops.

I think God has perfect timing, and I love it. Not a moment before I was ready did he call me back to him. And as I came to the realization that I needed to learn how to come down off the mountaintop, he sent me a few readings in a book I was working through. Each day of the year it has a different reading, and the very next day after painfully limping down a mountainside, the reading talked about that very topic. Chambers pointed out that we're not meant to live our lives on the mountaintops. Those amazing times of mountaintop views are meant to change us, so we can better live in the valley.

I thought my life was going to be so easy now that I was restored to relationship with God. I wasn't sure God was real, so he showed me. I still doubted; he showed me more. I wasn't sure where to go in the fall, so he showed me. For some reason I just pictured my life continuing on in this closeness and clarity with God. Then, when it didn't, I tumbled down into the valley of my old life. I stopped hearing and feeling God's closeness. I fell into old habits. I didn't know how to talk about what happened. I needed to learn how to come down from the mountain better.

Reading and understanding the Bible isn't something we're meant to do with our own minds. It's meant to be done with the help of God. I still don't understand much of what's written in the Bible, but I've realized that being changed on the mountaintops, coming down with the right perspective, and just continuing to move higher and deeper, is all that matters. I don't *need* to underline stuff. I just need to grow in relationship with Jesus, and he'll use the Bible to teach me.

In his perfect timing.

Chapter Twenty-One

I have a friend, Val, who gives the best hugs ever. She squeezes tightly, and holds on for just a few extra seconds. Normally I'd have released my hug, but she's still holding on, those few extra seconds that say, "I love your friendship!" I love Val hugs. As I hugged Luke good-bye before he flew back to Canada, it brought tears to my eyes. I knew it would. We had just walked 800 km from the south of France all the way across Spain. We had shared in one of the most incredible experiences, and made a memory that will definitely last a lifetime. Luke was flying west, back to Canada, and the next day I'd be back at the airport getting on a flight myself, heading east, to Thailand. I wasn't sure what the next adventure would hold for me, but I knew I'd be missing Luke.

As we walked across Spain on the Camino de Santiago, we grew closer to each other and closer to Jesus. We would walk about twenty-five kilometers a day, we carried all our belongings in packs on our backs, and we shared some amazing time of iron sharpening iron. As we inched our way across the map of Spain, we also inched our way through a 40-day devotional book, and talked and prayed with each other every day. After our amazing trip was over, we came to the realization that the longest we had spent apart from each other in the past thirty days was about thirty minutes. And we didn't even want to kill each other!

I was thinking about relationships in my life and how blessed I am to have such incredible friends. I can be a pain in the ass sometimes, and having a friend who suffers from depression isn't easy. As I let people into my inner circle of friends, of those I love and trust, I'll share with them about my struggle with this illness. It's hard for people to understand and respond to. Luke is one of my favorite people in the world, he's got so much patience, he's willing to just go on crazy adventures like I am, and he's got a heart that is pure gold.

I started to make friends with Jesus.

I began to wonder how my Christianity would be different this time around. It's so easy to fall into the "Christian lifestyle." Going to church on Sunday, maybe join a small group, talk the talk, mentor others, do things for his kingdom. It's all fine and good, but none of that helped me when I was younger. I knew that what needed to be different was relationship. I had no real relationship with Jesus before. I would say things like, "I'll pray for you" in order to sound wise, deep, and spiritual. Then I'd just forget. I'd preach the gospel, but if anything it was more about other people having a connecting, defining moment with God than me having one. If things were going to be different, it had to be relationship first.

How do you have a relationship with Jesus?

I started to wonder how I could have a relationship with a person I couldn't see. I put the thought in the back of my brain where I let questions simmer and then moved on with life. Spending every day with Luke helped show me the answer. I was searching for a secret recipe on how to "befriend Jesus" when the answer was right in front of me. I just need to be myself.

I've said it before—I'm pretty relationally handicapped. My friendships are so important to me, it's not a bad thing, but sometimes it causes me pain. I find a new friend, and I jump into their lives with both feet. I love my friends, and I'm sure they love me back. If a friend is struggling with something, I'll jump on a plane and go visit them. If I can't physically go and make them laugh then I'll send them a card, a book, an email, or a text message just telling them they're awesome. I love to make my friends smile. Love does stuff, remember. This is a fun way to live life. I spend more money with Air Canada than I probably should (or have), but my friends are worth it. How I become friends with Jesus is the same.

Luke and I would pray together each day we were on the Camino, and I love to listen to Luke pray. I really believe you can tell a lot about a person's relationship with Jesus by listening to them pray. If they pray, "Dear great and glorious Jesus in the stained glass," rather than "hey Jesus, my friend," then you know there is more religion than relationship. I'm not into religion one bit. I'm into relationship. One of the first things I noticed about how Luke prays is that he tells God how cool things are. He'll say things like, "God, thank you for letting me spend time with my friends today; it was so cool to be able to see them again." I used to pray similar prayers, but I'd only say the first part, thanking God for something, but then I'd forget to tell him it was cool.

God wants to know how cool things are.

I realized that I make friends by sharing stories with them (and I've got a lot of stories), making them laugh, traveling with them, being generous with my time, money, possessions, wisdom, and asking questions. Sometimes my friends get annoyed because I ask so many questions, but I just like to make them talk. So I suddenly realized that's what I need to do with Jesus. Why should I try to change the formula? That would only make it religious. I'd tell my friends that I was thankful to get to hang out with them, but then I'd continue and tell them how cool it was. I'd recount stories and moments, and laugh about it. Why not do that with Jesus? He loves to laugh with us. I had to learn how to pray in a new way, a less religious way, and a more personal way. Jesus loves to meet us in those moments and say things back to us like, "Yeah, that was cool, wasn't it?"

I had to learn to ask questions of Jesus. I realized that so often when we talk to him we're telling him stuff. We're telling him what we want, we're telling him what's on our mind and heart—and there is nothing wrong with that. But I realized that I ask my friends a ton of questions, but I don't know if I've ever asked Jesus a question. The beautiful thing about this is that when you ask a question, you usually shut up and listen for an answer. I think sometimes when we pray we talk too much and don't listen enough. I love asking my friends questions because it gets them talking, it gives me insight into their lives. Why wouldn't I want Jesus to talk to me? Why wouldn't I want to gain some insight into Jesus' life or will for my life? Sometimes he never tells me because I'm too busy talking and not willing to spend time listening. Now when I pray I try to ask Jesus a question or two, and then I just sit quietly for a while and listen. Sometimes when I listen I only get silence, but you'd be surprised how often you ask a question and actually get an answer back. The other thing I love about questions is that I believe asking questions about someone shows you care and are interested in them. I want my questions to be a form of worship to Jesus.

I started to wonder about traveling with Jesus. I love to travel with my friends, go on adventures with them, and it dawned on me that why not do this same thing with Jesus? A guy's weekend, just the two of us. Iron sharpening iron with Jesus! I started to ask myself if I'm being generous with my time, money, and possessions. Am I sharing those things with Jesus? When I went into Burma, I attended a church service in a small village. Maybe only 10 families in the whole village, and they were all dirt poor. They slept on bamboo mats on the floor of their huts, and they ate rice for breakfast and dinner—they couldn't afford to have three meals a day. Yet, when it came time to take up an offering at church, every man, woman, and child gave something. I was moved to tears to see it. Even if they were just putting in the equivalent of a penny, because it was all they had, they put something in. Even the toddlers that were running around each had a coin or even a rock to put into the basket. It was so humbling, and made me really question how generous with my money and possessions I really am.

Jesus loves to sit with us while we're talking with him, while we're being generous with our time, money, possessions, and wisdom. He loves to leave us with a feeling of a Val hug when we say Amen. The feeling of someone telling you, through their hug, that they love your friendship.

Chapter Twenty-Two

Jesus and I have an inside joke. I don't like to say I hear Jesus talking to me. I think it sounds a bit strange, maybe even a bit pretentious, but I hear Jesus talking to me. It's not talking like a voice from heaven, or a burning bush, or an angel standing at my bedside. It's a thought that comes into my head, randomly, speaking *to* me, rather than from me, and always something I wouldn't have necessarily thought myself. One could argue that it's just my subconscious responding to my emotional state—but I like to think it's Jesus talking to me, making jokes with me. He's cool like that.

I have inside jokes with many of my close friends. Sometimes they're really dumb, sometimes it's an ongoing prank, or sometimes it's just a single word that we'll both look at each other and laugh about. My friend Mike used to drive me around when we were both posted to CFB Edmonton. Whenever we were driving somewhere or getting in or out of the car, I would flip on his seat heaters.

There were multiple occasions when he would drop me off somewhere, and a few minutes later my phone would buzz, I would smile, knowing it's him texting me to tell me I'm an idiot for turning on his seat heater. It never ceased to make me laugh picturing him driving away, and then suddenly starting to squirm as his back and butt started to heat up, until finally, with a grunt he would realize I'd done it again. I love it. Mike's awesome.

My aunt and I always laugh whenever we talk about girls. One time I was describing what I wanted in a girlfriend or wife, and one thing I said is I want a girl who is flexible. What I meant when I said that was, because my career and life were so crazy and all over the place, that she should be flexible to move around the world and go on adventures with me. What my aunt thought I meant was that it was very important for me to have a girlfriend who can touch her toes. Now anytime we are talking about a potential girl, we both crack up laughing because we ask if she can touch her toes. It's totally stupid, but we literally will laugh until we cry sometimes. She's the best.

The thing that I love about inside jokes is that you really need to trust, know, and love the person you're sharing that joke with. You don't often share inside jokes with strangers or people you don't like, or Ned Flanders who sits a few pews in front of you. You share them with people who know your heart, who love your stupidity and humor, and who love to laugh. My friend Brett and I laugh all the time when we're together. Sometimes we'll start laughing at the other person's laugh, and then that makes them laugh even more, which then makes the other person laugh even more. One time I had to pull my car over because I couldn't see the road anymore due to the tears of laughter streaming down my face.

When Jesus made an inside joke with me it was one of the most incredible moments of my life; the power, beauty, and grace of Jesus coming through in his perfect humor. Luke was in the bunk bed above me, and he was worried because he thought I was sobbing, but I was just trying to laugh quietly so people wouldn't think I was insane for laughing out loud randomly. I was struggling with some stuff, I had shared it with Luke, and then I went to bed, worried how my night might spiral. Previously I had explained to Luke sometimes I had these negative, self-defeating thoughts come into my mind, and I would be fighting them off like a Ninja Turtle fighting the Foot Clan. Like I'd be kicking butt, tossing Foot Clan every which way, but no matter which direction I'd turn there would be another one coming, and then another and another. As I was lying in bed, worried about my struggling thoughts, with a heavy, sad heart, I prayed to Jesus that he could give me strength to fight the Foot Clan and then suddenly Jesus said to me, "Can I be Raffy?" I busted out laughing. It was so amazing. It was perfect on so many levels.

When we were kids we used to pretend to *be* people. When we'd play road hockey we'd say, "I'm Wayne Gretzky," or, "I'm Patrick Roy." Or we'd say, "Can I be Mario Lemieux today?" So for Jesus to say, "Can I be Raffy?" was so classic because he knew I'd know exactly what he was talking about. The other beautiful part about all this was he knew that my favorite Ninja Turtle was Donny, so I think he knew that it would be cool if he were Raffy. (Also, if you know anything about the Ninja Turtles, and anything about Jesus, you can see why he'd pick Raffy.)

As I lay there laughing, I just had this picture of me and Jesus, back to back, with the Foot Clan coming from all sides, and we would just kick butt all night. Kicking butt and taking names, all night long. I said to Jesus, "If we're going to do this, we're going to do it together. Wherever I go, you're coming." And he did. We spent a few minutes kicking negative thoughts out of my heart and brain, and then I felt so peaceful. I had tears streaming down my face because I was so moved with emotion after laughing with Jesus. It was my first inside joke with Jesus.

I lay there, trying to fall asleep, listening to my music, when suddenly Jesus said, "Shhh, listen to the cello here, this is my favorite part." I was amazed. I had recruited my butt-kicking partner to come with me to fight negative thoughts, but now that that was finished, he still wanted to hang out with me. I was listening to some piano music that I have listened to many, many times before - but suddenly I heard the cello. I had never noticed it before. But I had told Jesus, "Wherever I'm going tonight, you're coming with me." He did. I went to my favorite sleepy-time piano music, and he came too. He even shared with me his favorite part of the song.

If I were to tell you some of the greatest moments in my life I would tell you about riding a Harley through the Italian Dolomites, I'd tell you about skydiving, I might tell you about my first kiss, or cross-country skiing across Lapland. But now, I might tell you about the time I literally laughed until I cried because of an inside joke with my friend Jesus.

Chapter Twenty-Three

We were coming in from a patrol exercise to the patrol base. It was around midnight, and our patrol had been a total disaster. We humped it about four kilometers away, did a reconnaissance of the objective, got bumped by artillery sims, paraflares, and thunder flashes, and then got lost on our way back to the patrol base. As we approached the patrol base, we paused to collect our hidden rucks about 200 meters from the base, when suddenly we heard all hell breaking loose back at the patrol base. The base was being attacked. As things started to sound like they were dying down, we made our way back to the patrol base. Our new platoon senior was getting screamed at by the staff, and we quickly fell into our formation. I was a machine gunner, so I was on a flanking point.

We made our way back into the forest to re-establish a patrol base. We formed a tight exploded cigar; I was at the twelve o'clock with the machine gun. My position was half in a puddle, and the other half in a thorn bush. It seemed that the temperature of the air started to drop as my adrenaline did. I was soaking wet from dew and sweat from our patrol, and soon I began to shiver. This was one moment when I asked myself why I wanted to join the army. Lying prone in a thorn bush and puddle, soaking wet, sleep deprived, and shivering. It was terrible.

I think that as God calls us back to him from an extended period away he does it gently. He won't grab hold of us and show us all of our terrible sin all at once, but rather he'll convict us gently. For me, the first thing that I felt convicted about, or that I should try to change, was my language. I swore like a sailor. I lived in a world of army dudes and hockey players - I'll let your imagination take it from there. But, I felt like I needed to try to not swear so much, and I was making a very conscious effort to tame my tongue. Then, the patrol bump happened.

I had an old coach that I used to work with who always told me that when the pressure gets turned up, everyone reverts back to his or her true colors. This made me sad because when I found myself being tested in a tough situation the first thing that happened was I let loose like a machine gun shooting curses out of my mouth. That night sitting in the thorn bush, being stabbed every time I moved an inch, I reverted to my true colors. I guess the only positive was at least now I recognized it.

The twelve o'clock or machine gunner's nest can be a lonely place. You're usually off on your own somewhere, often forgotten about until you're needed or in trouble. As I lay there in total misery, shivering, trying to stay awake, my buddy Mike crawled over to me and lay down beside me. Mike and I weren't overly close, but the thing about Mike is he's got a heart of gold, and will do anything to help his fellow soldiers out. Mike lay down next to me and started asking me how I was doing and just talking to me. He started laughing when he saw my body convulsing with shivers, and he crawled away and came back with his ground sheet, which he covered us both under. He asked me if I knew why we were still in such a tight position instead of expanding to a more comfortable position and taking turns on picket. I had no idea, and I'm sure I expressed that with a few swear words.

My respect for Mike grew leaps and bounds that night. Eventually the shivering slowed down; I don't think it ever stopped, but it got a bit better. Mike and I each took a turn manning the gun while the other got a few minutes sleep. Mike is now a great friend whom I make an effort to go visit when I can. It's fun to show up at his place, see his wife and beautiful daughter, and share dinner and a beer. There is a bond between soldiers that is really special, a brotherhood. I want to feel that way about Jesus.

The thing is, I think Mike did exactly what Jesus does. When we're having the worst night of our lives, sitting in a thorn bush, soaking wet, freezing to death, Jesus crawls up beside us and sits in the thorns and puddle with us. When we're out on the twelve o'clock position, all alone, we can count on Jesus to be there with us, willing to lie down beside us to keep us warm, or at least alive. And I think the coolest part is, when we're in those terrible nights with the pressure turned up, and we revert back to our true colors, letting loose every swear word we know, or, just being the sinners that we are, Jesus doesn't leave. In fact those are the times that he moves in closer and says, "Here, let me take a turn on the gun; you take a few minutes sleep."

Mike was right there beside me, and I love him for it. But if I can start to look for and see Jesus in the dark places in my life, then I wonder if I'll begin to experience him like the brotherhood of soldiers. That unspeakable bond that you know is there as you make eye contact across the table and take a sip of your beer.

Chapter Twenty-Four

When I was getting myself kicked out of the Baptist church that I had grown up in, the minister came to my home to try to get me to apologize. He tried to guilt me into apologizing—my head was a bit too hard for that. He told me that the end days are near, that soon the world would be destroyed and I needed to live right. He asked me to think about the seniors who came to our church. He said he imagined them sitting in the back rows wringing their bony hands thinking about when death will come. He may have been a bit melodramatic, but he did a good job sucking all the joy out of Christianity and his church. If I were the minister of a church and my congregation was sitting there wondering when they're going to die, I'd consider putting a bit more life into my messages. Maybe a bit more Life, with a capital "L".

I love the joy of Jesus. He loved kids, he loved to laugh, and I even imagine he loved to dance. In the story when Jesus turns the water into wine, as John Eldredge points out, he didn't only make a bit of wine, but the clay pots that were brought to him filled to the brim with water. Each pot held about twenty-five gallons of water. If you do the math, Jesus made close to 800 bottles of wine. My friend Luke pointed out that at these wedding celebrations in Jesus' day, usually the whole village or community came out. So maybe 800 bottles of wine doesn't go as far as if I were to have 800 bottles of wine at my wedding—but I can picture the scene, Jesus laughing, dancing, celebrating the beauty of marriage, and then giving them enough wine to keep the party rocking all night. And not just any old wine, the finest- quality wine. Man, he is so generous. Who wouldn't want to be friends with this guy?

I have a stubborn streak in me. I think I got it from my grandpa. He was one of my favorite guys in the world. I used to love to sit on his lap and listen to him tell stories about the adventures he had been on. Whenever my grandpa came to visit, we were never allowed to sit beside each other at the dinner table because of the trouble we would cause. My grandpa never sat around rubbing his hands wondering when death would come—he lived every minute of his life with full-throttle passion. Sometimes not everyone around him wanted to go the same crazy speed he wanted to go, and he'd stubbornly just go off on his own. I do the same thing.

When my grandpa was too old to drive, they replaced his car with one of those old-folks electric scooters. It had two speeds, turtle speed and rabbit speed. I don't think my grandpa ever went turtle speed. My grandpa used to zip along roads and trails, and when people wouldn't move out of his way he'd beep his little scooter horn at them. But that horn sucked; it didn't let people know he was coming. So he went down to the sporting goods store and bought an air horn and taped it to the front of his scooter. So when he'd speed around the trail and come up behind someone, he'd blast the air horn at them, and then bound by at rabbit speed. I'm sure he'd be laughing to himself for half the day replaying their reactions as he drove by, his white hair breezing in the wind.

My grandpa knew the love that Jesus had. I'm sure he's up there in heaven going rabbit speed, making Jesus laugh. My grandpa never sat around waiting for death; rather, he embraced life. I try to live like my grandpa, and sometimes it makes other people furious, but I usually snicker about it as I bound by.

Sometimes my stubbornness has caused me to get into trouble, and I'm sure sometimes hurt God. I've heard God calling me, asking me to do something, and I flat-out say no. To think, the audacity, the nerve. There have been times when I haven't wanted to soften my heart to God's calling, nudging, or scripture. I may have read a verse and just said to myself that I'm not going to follow that particular verse.

I've come to realize, though, that surrendering myself is an art. It's not something that I just can do. It takes years of practice, refining, and failed attempts. An artist doesn't just pick up a brush today and paint a masterpiece. He or she usually has many failed first attempts. Softening my heart and listening to Jesus calling me isn't going to happen just like that. Sometimes when Jesus calls us, he gently comes up behind us and beeps his horn, other times he blasts an air horn to get our attention. Sometimes we ignore his beeping, or get furious that he scared us, but I'm sure Jesus laughs to himself as we try to do things on our own strength, with our own stubborn hearts.

> "In my vision at night I looked, and there before me was one like a son of man, coming with the clouds of heaven. He approached the Ancient of Days and was led into his presence. He was given authority, glory and sovereign power; all nations and peoples of every language worshiped him. His dominion is an everlasting dominion that will not pass away, and his kingdom is one that will never be destroyed."
>
> — DANIEL 7:13-17

His kingdom will never be destroyed. God doesn't need me for anything. He doesn't need me to be a good person so his Kingdom will grow or be sustained. He doesn't need me to go and convert everyone to be a Christian. His kingdom will never

ever be defeated—whether I believe in it or not. All nations and peoples of every language will worship him. It's not up to me to get 'er done. His kingdom and his plans are going to happen with or without me, if I believe or don't believe. If I listen to him and say no; if I have a hard heart or soft heart for people and his word. It makes no difference to the grand plans–he's already won!

When I let go of trying to do things for Jesus, and instead accept that he doesn't need me for anything—yet still personally died for me—it makes me *want* to have a soft heart, it makes me *want* to listen to his calling, it makes me *want* to obey. When I figure it out in my heart that his kingdom will be just fine without me, but he still loved me enough to kick the devil's butt on my behalf, it makes me *want* to be joyful about this life I have to live, not sit around waiting for death to come.

Chapter Twenty-Five

I grew up as a small-town country boy, with acres of forest as my backyard, boats and snowmobiles, tree forts and camping trips. Endless outdoor adventures were the backdrop of my childhood and continue to be a big part of my life today.

I remember sitting in my trench in the army during a training exercise, staring up at my small square of sky that I could see without lifting my head out of the trench. I could see commercial airliners crisscrossing the sky. Their trails would cross the sky like the track plan of our defensive position. I would wonder who was on those planes and wonder where they were going. The airport has been such a big part of my adult life. Every time I would be in the lounge awaiting boarding, I would always be excited about the journey. Going somewhere new. Going to see a friend.

Wandering.

No matter where I go, I always love to spend time outside in nature. In England I love to go walking in the Dales outside Leeds, or you can find me sitting by the pond in Hyde Park. In Italy there is so much beauty everywhere I go; the mighty peaks of the Dolomites stretching to the sky. In Finland getting out of the city to a friend's cottage is always a highlight for me; it's always so quiet, so peaceful.

When I was living the darkness of a Finnish winter, I was really struggling. I flew to England for a week to visit my friend Tom. On my last day before I returned to Finland, he took me on a long hike. We were about an hour outside Leeds, and we ended up at the lookout point. We sat down and didn't say anything. We just took in the Dales stretching out before us; beautiful countryside, rolling hills, and walking trails crisscrossing the fields. Eventually Tom broke the silence and said to me, "I know you're returning to a difficult place, but I wanted to bring you here so you can remember this beauty when you're having a hard time in the Finnish winter." And every time after that when I was struggling, I would just picture the view from that rock, looking out over the fields and forests. It was beautiful.

Then, when it came time to leave Finland a few years later, a country I had grown to love so much, my friend Tatu did the same thing. He took me and our group of friends to his cottage. In true Finnish style we fished, smoked cigars, and enjoyed the sauna and a swim in the chilly lake water. We sat for hours talking, laughing, and watching the sun slowly dip down. Around midnight we all sat down for a massive feast for dinner, the endless daylight from the Northern sun glowing through the windows still. My friends presented me with a gift they had all chipped in to buy, a necklace from a famous Finnish designer. It was really amazing. But then Tatu took me outside and we stood by the water sharing a cigar, watching the sun paint the water red and orange, and he said the same thing Tom had said, "When you think of Finland, I want you to remember this," and he motioned out to the calmness of the lake.

Falling in love with Jesus is a really amazing experience. As I was reading *The Beautiful Outlaw* by John Eldredge, he challenged the reader to start saying, "I love you Jesus," throughout the day. His challenge was that every time you see something beautiful, tell Jesus you love Him. This simple statement honestly will change your life. At first it was a bit difficult, and in all honesty, it felt a bit strange to talk about, and think about saying, "I love you" to another man. But as I started to get to know Jesus better it was hard not to love him.

Now there isn't a day that goes by that I don't see the beauty of Jesus in creation. Maybe it's a sunny day that I'm enjoying, and once I realize I'm happy to feel the sun on my face I'll say, "Jesus, I love you." Or maybe it's the way trees line a road, providing shade. Maybe it's breathtaking views from mountaintops, or a sunset of a million colors. Maybe it's a powerful thunderstorm rolling in, or the way a bird floats effortlessly through a breeze. God created all these things so we could enjoy it. He created it all, and then said, "It is good."

Each time I think of Finland, I picture Tatu's cottage. I can smell the cigar smoke hovering in the air, I can feel the bite of the spring air, and I can sense the stillness of the water. I can hear my friends' laughter. I know Jesus paints these canvases especially for us. I know he is there, standing nearby, maybe leaning against a tree, watching me, watching the sunset, and saying to himself, "Yup, it *is* good."

Chapter Twenty-Six

I have a friend named Wah Shee. He's just a young guy, but he taught me a lot about Jesus, my faith, and joy. I met Wah Shee at the hospital in Chiang Mai, Thailand. Wah Shee is seventeen years old, from Karen State in Burma. He had been walking along a makeshift bamboo bridge when it broke with him on it. His leg slipped down through a gap in the bridge boards, and then the ropes that were suspending the bridge snapped under the tension, causing the bridge to twist like a corkscrew, with Wah Shee's leg still stuck in the middle. As the bridge twisted, it snapped Wah Shee's leg in multiple places, instantly sending one of his leg bones pushing out through the skin.

Wah Shee was dragged from the wreckage, his bone still protruding, and him nearly unconscious from the pain. They brought him back into the village, deep in the Burma jungle, where he remained for two weeks. Two weeks with a bone sticking out of his leg. Two weeks without seeing a doctor or medic or getting a painkiller. Wah Shee told me, in his amazing broken English, how one of the village elders tried to push the bone back into his leg. Wah Shee said, "This was a pain number ten and I sleep." Meaning he passed out because the pain was so intense.

With the help of a few incredible organizations, Wah Shee got carried through the jungle and eventually transported to Chiang Mai, where I met him. At first they thought they were going to cut his leg off; infection had set in and eaten away most of his bone and muscle. They put him onto a vacuum pump system that sucks out the infection, and with lots of time and prayer, his leg started to heal.

I would go and visit Wah Shee in the hospital every day. I felt bad for him. If I were a seventeen-year-old boy trapped in a hospital with eight roommates, I'd want a visitor too. Wah Shee and I became friends. We learned to play some games, and we'd kill ourselves laughing together trying to catch the other cheating. I would hold his hand as he would wince through the pain of the doctors changing the dressings on his leg or taking out or putting in pins. We would nudge each other anytime a cute nurse would come into the room, and then laugh about it when she would catch us staring. Wah Shee became more of a joy to my life than I probably was in his.

Wah Shee can't speak English very well, so I asked him if he'd teach me Karen, his mother tongue. So I would write down some simple sentences: "This is an apple." "The apple is red." "Can I have an apple?" And Wah Shee would translate them into Karen and then laugh at me as I'd butcher the pronunciation. It was fun.

It got me thinking about Jesus. Jesus became fully man; he had to be taught how to speak the same as me. I pictured Mary and Joseph sitting with Jesus saying, "This is an apple. Can you say apple?" The One who hung the stars in the sky, and knows each one by name. When you think of Jesus this way, instead of as a superhero, it really makes the relationship seem deeper, and the love of sacrifice more real. The One who learned to say, "The apple is red," eventually said, "Father, forgive them."

After Wah Shee had been in the hospital for a few months, and he and I had become friends, I found out that his funding had fallen through. When patients like Wah Shee are brought out of Burma, they're sponsored by an NGO or aid organization that "guarantees" the hospital that the bill will be paid. Then they apply to organizations in the western world for funding support. Wah Shee, we found out, didn't meet the criteria of one organization because they wanted him to fly to America so they could do the surgery there. The problem is, Wah Shee and his father have no papers: no passports, birth certificates, or driver's licences. They live in the jungle. When we were checking in Wah Shee and we were asked when his birthday was, no one knew. His father searched his memory banks and came up with, "I think it was sixteen or seventeen years ago, and I think he was born in the summer." So we just made up a birth date for him. It's not as easy as just getting him a passport and flying him to America.

So we were left scrambling. His bill was already over $8000 US dollars, or a quarter of a million Thai Baht. I was talking with one of our medics about this situation and what happens if we can't find funding. She said, "God will provide." It sounds like a nice sentiment, and one I was praying for every day. Then she told me about a similar patient, one she had grown very fond of, who also lost the funding. She told me she put the whole bill on her credit card, around $6000, and trusted God that he'd provide. Wow! I thought about it for a while, and I realized that it was putting a dollar value on your faith in God. How much faith did I have in God? Did I have a thousand-dollar faith? Faith that if I put a grand on my credit card, God could provide for me to pay it back, but any more than that and it would be irresponsible? Or maybe I have $2000 faith. Or maybe like Mon, our medic, $6000 faith, but any more would just be crazy. Do I have $8000 faith to pay for Wah Shee's hospital bill?

How much is a leg worth? How much would you pay for your right leg? Maybe if I were fifty years old and had gotten a lot of miles out of my leg, I'd part with it a little easier. But what if my seventeen-year-old son was going to lose his leg... how much would I pay then? Would I pay $8000 so my son could keep his leg? Of course! That almost sounds like too good of a deal. What about my friend? Would I pay $8000 for my friend to keep his leg? It's such an impossible decision to make.

Wah Shee brings so much joy into my life. It's hard to feel sad about yourself after you visit him. His smile lights up the room, and he sits up and stretches out his hand to shake yours as soon as he sees you coming. He has days when he is in lots of pain, but he still smiles when he says, "Today, much pain." He loves to tell me about how much he loves to climb trees, play sports with his friends, especially soccer, and be outside. On weekends I'd put him in a wheelchair and take him outside in the back of the hospital. He would just sit and stare at the birds, the trees, and the sun. He would smile when he would feel the wind on his face and smell the air. You could see him coming alive, like a tiger that had been released from captivity. It was amazing to watch.

As I hemmed and hawed about his hospital bill, Mon gently reminded me that, "God will provide." I was wincing as she said it, but then she continued, "And maybe sometimes what he'll provide is a lot of hard work and a steady job you can go to work at." It brought tears to my eyes.

Sometimes I expect God to provide a huge miracle, like an $8000 cheque to show up in my mailbox to pay for my friend's leg. And it's not unlike God to do that—but other times, God just wants us to work hard. He'll provide us with a nine-to-five job, and he'll say, "Here, go to work, pay your bills." I think Christianity feels better with dirty hands and after a long day of work.

Chapter Twenty-Seven

God will talk to you if you're willing to listen. When I was young I never heard God talking to me, but the more I get to know his voice, his character, and the way he speaks, the more I can hear him. Like the young Samuel who hears the Lord speaking to him for the first time, he keeps running to Eli saying "here I am, you called me" and after the third time Eli, who knows the voice of God tells Samuel to listen again, and if he hears the voice calling him that it is God. And when Samuel hears the voice again, he says "Speak, for your servant is listening"

Last night I was feeling disconnected and that I need to spend some time with God. I had some big decisions that needed to be made and I wasn't sure how to make them. I knew in my heart that I hadn't been spending enough time talking with God lately and that really the answers to my questions lay with him. So I dedicated my evening to spending time with my Lord. I went for a run and I put on some praise and worship music while I ran. It was a great time of worship and just loving God. Then when I got back to my room I went and found a quiet area and I just started to read my Bible. I prayed and while I was praying I asked Jesus a question. I asked him what he thought of me. When I opened my eyes I pictured Jesus lounging in the chair across from me, just sitting quietly in the chair watching me, contemplating how to answer. He was sitting sideways, his legs resting over one of the arms of the chair. I closed my eyes again with hopes I would hear his answer. Silence.

As I finished up my evening and got myself into bed I prayed again; "God, I want to give you my dreams tonight and just ask for a peaceful sleep. I love you" and then I was out cold. Now one thing you should know about me is that I never dream, maybe once or twice a year I'll wake up and know I had been dreaming or be able to remember my dreams, but this particular night I was almost immediately in the most colorful, vivid dream.

I was sitting in the passenger seat of a convertible; it was an old classic convertible, the kind with big leather bench seats, no seatbelts, kind of like what Johnny Cash would drive. I'm not sure who was driving, but we were going a decent clip down the highway, and I could feel the wind in my hair from the top down. It was warm. I was angry about something; what was it? We were late. I hate being late, I was supposed to be somewhere, to see someone, and we were running behind schedule and I was annoyed. I was texting with them, saying, "We're almost there." We pulled off the highway; I wasn't really paying attention, just staring out the side of the car as we pulled up the driveway. There were huge wooden doors that two people pushed open as we approached. At first, I didn't pay any attention to who they were, but as we drove past, I noticed they were my friends. I was confused, wondering why they were there? We drove into the courtyard of the house. There was a huge roundabout paved with bricks. As we made our way around the roundabout, I noticed it was lined with people, all my friends. My friends from Finland were all standing there smiling and laughing, my Italian friends were there, my friends from all across Canada were there, my friends from Thailand and England were all there, my brothers and parents were there, my Godchildren were playing with my nephew, and a lot of my old players were there. As we slowly drove around the roundabout, I realized I was driving into a surprise birthday party for myself, and all my friends had traveled all across the world to be there.

I began to get choked up, I was so overwhelmed with joy, with happiness, with thankfulness, I couldn't believe someone had planned this for me, that all my friends had journeyed so far to be there for me, and that people hadn't forgotten my birthday. My anger for being late was replaced with a smile on my face, and just as overwhelming tears of joy spilled over, Jesus leaned over from the driver's seat and said, "Want to know what I think of you, David? David, you're a surprise party for me; you're that feeling of overwhelming joy and fullness in my heart."

I woke up instantly.

I felt the warmth of Jesus like a blanket around me. I knew it was from him, I knew it was his unique, personal voice. I looked at my clock. I had only been asleep for two hours, and normally if dreams happen at all for me, they happen right before dawn, so I knew this dream was from Jesus. I began to think about it more, and I realized that not only did it fill me with so much awe and joy, but it also quietly revealed a wound I have.

It's a bit embarrassing to admit, but I've always wanted a surprise party planned in my honor; a really good one, where I have no clue, and people have come from all corners of the globe. I want to feel appreciated. The thought of someone planning a surprise party for me would just make me feel so loved, so full, and so valued. So for Jesus to clearly tell me that he thinks of me like a surprise party means so much to me. But it also reveals more of the character and voice of Jesus to me. Jesus doesn't come to us with rules, and thou shall and thou shall nots. He comes to us with so much creativity, he's so original and personal, and I love that Jesus was in on the surprise party the whole time!

Look at the way Jesus is in the Bible, he never does the same thing twice, he never heals a person or speaks to a person the same way twice, he is unique and personal with each person he comes into relationship with. He's like that today.

Every time I hear Jesus speaking to me it floors me, it makes my heart skip a beat and I am always at a loss for words. He doesn't say much, but the words that he says, I know it's him, and just a few words are always enough to totally change my world.

What does Jesus think of me? He thinks of me like a surprise party, and when he thinks of me he feels overwhelming joy and fullness. Wow. What an amazing friend. This is the God of the universe, the King of angel armies, the one who knows the number of stars in the sky and grains of sand on a beach. He's my friend, he loves me, and that brings me so much confidence. Confidence that relationship with him is all that matters, that learning to hear his voice is all that matters.

Ask questions to Jesus when you spend time with him. Ask him what he thinks of you. I promise you that when you hear the answer, it will be unique, personal, and just for you.

Chapter Twenty-Eight

I once read that depression is a conspiracy. The illness saps strength, and beating the illness takes huge strength. Sometimes more strength than we have. One thing I've learned about depression and Christianity is that the two don't always go hand in hand. Depression makes you doubt; it makes you talk and think negatively about yourself. It makes you feel embarrassed and shameful about how you're feeling. I don't know the number of times that I've woken up the morning after a fight with depression and felt embarrassed or shameful because of how I acted or what I shared with a friend.

A depression hangover.

Christianity is about believing in what you can't see. Having faith in love. So when you're being beaten down by negative self-talk and negative thoughts, believing in anything is hard. I find that when I am fighting depression, the last thing I want to do is read my Bible. Sometimes I pray out in agony, asking God to help me; sometimes I curse the heavens. Sometimes I run.

About a month after I left the army posting in Edmonton, I returned to visit friends on base. Enough time had passed to allow my emotions about the place to relax a bit. As I was driving down the highway towards base I passed the track that I used to run on.

I was flooded with all the emotions and memory of the times I'd spent running around the track, cursing at God. I felt the pain again, as if I were going through it all again.

Sometimes we need to revisit old places of pain.

I have an old journal that I have kept but never looked at. I know that in it is a lot of pain. When I started to keep that journal I was in my early twenties and trying to figure out why I couldn't control how I was feeling. At this point in my life I hadn't been diagnosed with depression; I really didn't know what depression was. But I knew I had something wrong with me. I had these intense mood swings; my logical mind would say one thing, but my emotions would say something else, and I'd take it out on my friends. I knew that in writing this book I would need to revisit that journal. I'd need to really dig into old places of pain to try and reflect on them. It's hard.

One of the first things that jumped out at me was how negative I was towards myself. I wrote several times things like, "They probably don't want to hang out with me," or "They'd probably be better off if I saved them the torture of my friendship." It's been many years since I wrote those words in my journal, but just like when I drove past CFB Edmonton, the emotions and memories flooded back quickly. The pain was real, as if I were there. While I didn't believe the words I wrote, I understood them.

I have heard hundreds of times the story of the prodigal son – but it wasn't until recently that the weight of that story really sank in for me. I realized that the son who took his inheritance early and spent it on parties and prostitutes probably had thoughts like I had. When he was working as a slave after all his money was gone, he probably thought about going home, but had thoughts of doubt, such as, "They probably don't want to see me." And then what happened? When he finally was at the lowest point he could get, realizing that the pigs were being treated better than he was, he humbled himself to go home.

When we visit these old places of pain, sometimes we'll be surprised what we find. When the prodigal son revisited his place of pain, it says his father saw him in the distance and *ran* to him. I am sometimes so afraid to revisit old places of pain, physical places, where I know I experienced pain ... Penticton, Edmonton, Kenora, Poland. The thought of going back to revisit the people and places where I felt so much pain, anger, and shame is terrifying. They're places where I was at the lowest points in my life. But I'm surprised how often when I revisit those places of pain, I'm met with someone running to forgive me. Our past is for reflection, not for residence. When satan reminds us of our past, we need to remind him of his future.

The thing about the prodigal son story that made me cry was the ending. The father throws a big party for his son who has returned, but his other son refuses to attend. The father goes outside to the pouting son, and asks him why he won't come in. The son explains that his brother took his inheritance, left, blew it all, and returned and he gets a party, yet he had been with the father the entire time, working hard for him, being a good son, and he never got a party. To which the father replies, "My son, you are always with me and everything I have is yours".

I never got it. I sided with the second son in this one. I think the brother is a punk; he made a dumb decision and he comes back and gets a party. I would be annoyed too, and I totally get the son pouting. But then I heard God ask me, "David, would you rather me throw you a party, or spend every day with me?"

I choose every day.

Chapter Twenty-Nine

In my book *The Wandering Leader*, I wrote a chapter on spirituality. If you read that chapter you would assume that I don't think very highly of the church, that I don't think very highly of God, and that I'm not a "Christian." And at the time I wasn't. I definitely wasn't living like a Christian; I was living like a good dude in the world. Focused on myself, my needs, money, and my career.

In preparation for this book I went back and I re-read that chapter. We grow so much in such a short time if we let ourselves. One thing that really stood out to me was how many times I used the word "religion." I probably used that word more times in that one chapter than I have in this entire book. It's what my faith was before, a religion. Today my faith is relationship and it's so different. It's so full, so fun, so energizing, and so joyful.

There are a couple things in that chapter that I might disagree with now, but some of the points I made I still would agree with, and for where I was in my life at that time, those words were true. I wondered if I wrote this book that I would need to change and re-publish that previous book with updated views, but I think that book is just fine, and for some people it will at least get them on the journey to find Truth.

Towards the end of the chapter on religion there was a paragraph that jumped out at me and brought tears to my eyes:

"There were a couple nights Luke and I debated religion and confidence until the sun was starting to come up, and as strange as it might sound, I really believe Luke was brought into my life for a reason; to show me that the work on my spirit isn't finished yet. That there is still more to come."

I just pictured God up in heaven chuckling to himself as I wrote those words years ago. The Luke I mention in that paragraph is the same Luke that is scattered throughout this book, one of my dearest friends. When I wrote those words I had no idea where I would be posted for my military training; I had no idea I'd get to know Luke and his entire family better. When I wrote those words Luke and I had only really communicated one or two times since leaving our basic army training. Yet, for some reason I felt like I needed to say it. Prophetic, in a way. Since that time Luke has become one of my best friends, we've traveled around Europe together, we walked 800 km across Spain, we've prayed together, we laughed and cried together, and we've grown as brothers.

Luke *was* brought into my life for a reason. When I met Luke years ago there was something in me that shouted out, "befriend this guy," so I did. Luke and I debated long into the nights on our basic training about religion, faith, and spirituality. I never conceded that he'd changed my mind or won the debate, but I think we both just enjoyed the subject. But to look back on it seems so incredible: it seems so undeniable that there was more at work than just two soldiers talking religion. The work on my spirit wasn't finished; there was still more to come. Lots more.

I can't help but smile at God's playfulness and love of a good caper. Recently Rainer and Val came to visit me while I was staying in Thailand. Val had a birthday while they were here. I love birthdays. I love doing things that are totally ridiculous and obnoxious on people's birthdays. When I was coaching in Italy, I used to decorate the players' equipment and stall in the dressing room. These were full-grown, tough, macho hockey men. I'd get a cake, I'd blow up balloons, I'd get streamers and I'd weave them through their stall and all their equipment. I'd put up a giant sign wishing them a happy birthday. They'd be annoyed if they weren't one of the first players at practice and had time to take down all this embarrassing stuff before the rest of the team arrived, but that's okay. So for Val, I had a caper planned.

I love a good caper.

The night before her birthday I told her I had something planned for the next day and that she needed to be ready to get up early and have an overnight bag prepared. At 5:00 a.m. I woke her up, and we headed to the airport. She still had no idea what was going on, and was kind of annoyed, she had just flown half way around the world and now was back at the airport. We checked in for our flights and made our way through security. Then we boarded our flights to Phuket, one of the most beautiful island resort areas in Thailand. We flew down there and met Jay who was living there. We spoiled Val for her birthday, for no other reason than to make her feel special and loved. It was great.

I don't think God is any different. I think he sometimes feels excited about a good caper. He knows the master plan, and sometimes it's more exciting to know the master plan than to be the one blurry eyed trying to figure out why you're in an airport. Sometimes it can actually be annoying being on the receiving end of a good caper, even if the end goal is to make you feel special and feel loved. It's annoying having to go places and do things that you're not sure why or what the big picture will be. But it's so much fun for the guy who knows the big picture, who sees how all the pieces of the puzzle will fit together, who can't wait for the sun to set and to see you smile and know that you feel loved! What's better than that?

I think God just loves that in our lives. I'm sure when I wrote those words about Luke and me in *The Wandering Leader* that he just smiled and rubbed his hands together. He knew the big picture; he knew that there was a caper in place, for nothing more than to make me feel special and to make me know Love. Luke was just a pawn in the caper, like the ticket agent at the airport, playing his part to bring me to realization of what's happening in my life. For a long time I was like Val, blurry eyed, stumbling my way through airport security, feeling a bit lost. That's okay, as long as there is someone loving who knows the big picture.

Chapter Thirty

I think as I moved along in God's plans for me; he brought me to Thailand and introduced me to incredible men and women of faith. He knew the hurt and the brokenness in my heart from Christians, and I think he wanted nothing more than to surround me with, as my mom says, Christians who are doing it right.

I thought back on the words that Pastor Greg had challenged me with as I boarded the flight from Heathrow to Chiang Mai: "Be all-in for Jesus." To which I responded, "I'm going to be all-out, until I can figure out how to be all-in." I had just finished walking 800 km across Spain, learning how to be all-in. Like most things in my life, I flew into Thailand with gusto and full of energy. I was now in with both feet, and I was going to take Chiang Mai by storm. I wanted nothing more than for people to see Christ in me, and to be a servant and blessing to the people I'd meet there. My first 48 hours in Chiang Mai saw me attend church, meet with the youth pastor, and ask to serve as a volunteer with the youth group, meet with the senior pastor to let him know I wanted to serve the church however I could, and join a small group of young adults to continue to grow and share my faith.

THE WANDERING BELOVED

I was all-in.

I think it's funny and so amazing how God brings people into our lives. When I was hurt and broken in Finland, God sent me Tom, who would become one of my best friends. When I was softening the ground of my heart, God sent Luke into my life to become a friend, a mentor, and a brother. And as God judged the season of my heart, he felt it was time for me to shake off some of the anger and shame towards "Christians" by introducing me to some of the best Christians in the world.

I decided to move to a new guesthouse after a couple weeks in Thailand, one that was recommended by people I was working with. So I moved to it, and was thankful for this nicer, cheaper place to stay. The next day my room was robbed, and all my money was stolen. 15,000 baht (about $500). Ouch.

This was one of the first times though that I could definitively say that God was changing me from the inside out. In my old life, I would have freaked out. I'd have called for a national investigation. I'd want the CIA, FBI, and all the king's horses and all the king's men to be investigating this petty break-in. But this time, I was totally calm. I tore my room apart searching for my envelope of money, but I never panicked, and in fact, the only thought I had was that someone could probably use that money more than I could. It was a shocking thought.

A few days later, one of my friends came up to me with his wife and took me aside. They said, "We heard you got broken into, and we want to help. Each month we put aside money in our budget just to give to people who need it." I was blown away. I tried to refuse their money, saying it was okay, and that they weren't rich and could use the money too. Jimmy just said, "Dude, you're gonna take this money one way or another, so either I'll beat it into your hand, or you can just take it." They gave me 6000 baht. What a blessing. How incredible is that?

A few weeks later I started to look for a new place to stay. I wanted a house to stay in during the month of December. I had friends coming from Canada to visit me, and I wanted to find a house that we could all rent for the month. I posted an ad in the church classified, saying that I was looking for a house for the month of December. A few days later, a lady emailed me saying her family was heading back to the USA for the holidays and if I didn't mind taking care of the cat, I could stay at their house for the month. I went and met with them for coffee to show them I wasn't totally crazy, and then a few weeks later went to look at the house.

As I walked in, I was blown away. It was a palace. The house was immaculate, with beautiful hardwood floors and more than enough space. There was a Christmas tree up, and the house was decorated with Christmas decorations. I was nearly choked up. I had been missing home; I had been missing the feeling of Christmas, of a decorated house and just feeling that Christmas-y feeling. She had decorated the house, even though they weren't going to be there at all for the holiday season. She had done it just to be a blessing to me.

I was floored by the blessings that Jesus can bring into our lives. Here was a family, handing the keys to their home to a nearly complete stranger. Why? Because I loved Jesus, and that was enough reference for them. Wow! That's doing it right.

I remembered reading Matthew 7:16:

"You can identify them by their fruit, that is, by the way they act. Can you pick grapes from thorn- bushes, or figs from thistles?".

You'll know them by their fruit. These are the Christians who are doing it right. These are the Christians that were melting my heart and restoring my faith. Earlier I reflected on Romans 1:16: "I'm not ashamed of the gospel." I realized I was ashamed of Christians. But in Thailand, I fully believe God was showing me Christians who were doing it right. Christians whom I was so blessed by. Like a couple that hosts a spaghetti dinner every Thursday night for volunteers. They don't want you to help clean up afterwards, or give any money. They just want to be a blessing and share their home and a meal with friends. They've been doing it every Thursday for twenty-five years!

But God doesn't just bless a little bit; he is so generous. He brought into my life so many people who are some of the most amazing Christians: Dave, our director, who lives Christ on the front lines of war-torn places. Mike, who showed me that it's okay for Christians, even ones in ministry, to have a beer, swear occasionally, and do it all with total overflowing love for Jesus. Adam, who would literally chase me around the office boardroom trying to fight me, all while we would be killing ourselves laughing. Christians who do love as an action word are the ones who change the world. They changed mine.

I can only hope and pray that as I grow in Christlikeness that my fruit will be a blessing to others. That people will know I'm a follower of Christ because of my fruit.

Chapter Thirty-One

Someone once told me that darkness doesn't just go away because we work at it. If we're in a place of total, utter darkness, no matter how hard we try, we can't create light. I can't screw a light bulb into my ear and think really hard. Light needs to come from somewhere else: a flashlight, electricity, or Jesus.

I always fear saying I'm cured of anything. I loved chewing tobacco, but I think that as I came back to the cross, Jesus wanted to show me how powerful he was. I was worried that I wouldn't be able to let go of the vices in my life, and as a result, wouldn't be "all-in," or a good Christian. Then Jesus took care of it. Without any desire or effort on my part I stopped chewing. Just like that. I carried around those containers of chewing tobacco that I had ordered from Sweden for six months. For the first two weeks, I carried an open tin in my pocket. But I never used it. Then I put it in my backpack, which I carry around with me everywhere I go. I brought six tins of snus with me to Europe, and three with me all the way down the Camino. I flew to Thailand and carried that snus with me the entire way. But not once did the desire return.

And then one day I realized I hadn't been drunk in months. Not by my strength at all. And it brings tears to my eyes to think about my brokenness and my darkness. It brings tears to my eyes when I think about my fight with depression, that since arriving in Thailand, and then returning back to Canada, I haven't had one day of uncontrollable darkness. A part of my life that normally comes in waves every few weeks was gone. And I'm so terrified to write those words, so full of doubt.

Doubt. Hello my old friend.

I know that I am weak, my flesh is weak, and my spirit is weak. I feel like if I write that I am cured of chewing tobacco and drunkenness, then I'm just going to fall off the wagon, hard. And it is scary, even inconceivable; to dream about saying I'm cured of depression. The fall hurts. But I think about my life, and how the sins in my life that I loved, that held me captive, were healed without effort. Even if I fall back into old habits and traps, and even if days of darkness come back, Jesus has shown me how powerful he is. He can take one look at me, drowning in waves of darkness, and calm the seas.

No matter how hard I try, I can't produce light. But darkness is always the prelude to light. When I was in Finland the physical darkness of a Finnish winter seeped into my bones. It was one of the only times that I have ever really felt what darkness feels like. I'm not talking about darkness as in evil; I'm talking about darkness as in a life that goes on without light in it. It's heavy; it's slow and tiring. It's sad. You can be lost in this darkness, where days blend together with night, where no matter how many layers of protection you put on to protect yourself from the cold, it will seep in. The darkness is stronger than the cold.

The cold will burn your skin, but the darkness will rot your bones. It will scar you from the inside.

There were so many days when I was lost in the darkness of my illness. Where it had seeped into my bones and was rotting me from the inside. Try as I might, I couldn't create light. I could try to live a good life, I could try to be moral and have some values, but those lights quickly run out of batteries or break. I could try to run away from the darkness with travel, distractions, or medicines. But I couldn't create light. Then Jesus said, "I am the light of the world. Whoever follows me will never walk in darkness, but will have the light of life."

I hate saying I'm cured of something, because then the pain of falling back into darkness is multiplied by the pain of my ego. Try as I might on my own to create light, it won't work. But now the light of the world lives in me. When I'm walking towards darkness, sometimes even intentionally, I can call upon the light in me, "Christ in me, I need you now."

Then the light shines.

Chapter Thirty-Two

The *Wandering Leader* was a book about dreaming, believing in yourself, and creating a life of excitement. I still love that book very much, and I think that there are lots of things in it that can help a person grow—but in looking back on it, I've realized that the book points the wrong way. The book points that "I" am the way. And now, with some disappointment in my life, I ask myself, well if Jesus is the way, then it means I can't be the way.

There are so many moments in my life when I am confident in my plans, in my dreams, and in my ability to conquer, that end up knocking me flat on my face. Poland was a dream come true for me: the head coach of a men's professional hockey team in Europe. Then, it all just blew up. Even when my agent was advising me against going there, my pride was telling me I'd make it work. Two lawsuits later, and with a totally broken heart and ego, I can chalk that up to a bad decision.

I spent a decade wandering the world. I drank a lot; I slept around a bit, and I tried to make myself the center of my universe. I tried to make myself a god. I grew a "following" online to buy my products, praise my books, and flood my inbox with worship-like emails. I would have sooner spit on a church than go into one, and I'd debate faith, religion, and Christianity all night long.

Then Jesus came into my life and showed me the real him. He showed me his power, his love, his tenderness, his light, and his grace. He showed me the characteristics that I was missing in my life. I tried to create power by having flashy business cards and books on the bestsellers' lists. I tried to find love in lustful relationships and one-night stands. I replaced tenderness with a hard, bitter heart. I lived in darkness, and I wouldn't accept grace from anyone unless I earned it. I came to God with anger and rage. I would run through the fields and trails with tears running down my face, swearing at him. I'm sure it broke his heart, but he never wavered in his plans of love for me.

As I was led to the cross, my logical, doubting mind couldn't rightly chalk it all up to coincidence. As I researched the lists and lyrics of worship songs, my heart was saying, "Just believe; you don't need to find the answers," but I didn't trust my heart, I didn't trust my mind or my body anymore. I knew that it would fade; I knew that it had deceived me in the past. When I doubt now, which I still do, I can remind myself that I'm one in 112 million. That God went way out of his way to organize that and show me that, for no other reason than to say, "David, I love you."

Whenever I hear Jesus speaking to me, he always calls me by name; he always calls me David. He never says 'Dave' or 'hey, pal'; he calls me David. And the name David means beloved. When I was young my mom gave me a bookmark for my Bible. At the top it said "David" and then it had this verse:

> "Let the *beloved* of the Lord rest secure in him, for he shields him all day long and the one the Lord loves rests between his shoulders."
>
> — DEUTERONOMY 33:12

THE WANDERING BELOVED

I am the beloved of the Lord.

I'm moved to tears by the power and love of the Lord. I'm shaken to the core of my life when I think that the one who spoke the world into existence took time out to plan a great caper for me. Oswald Chambers says, "Worship is giving God the best he has given you." God has given me life and light, so all I can do is humbly fall on my face and say, I'm all yours, God.

My God isn't the God of religion or Pharisees. My God is the God who will literally write the pages of history so that he can show you he loves you. My God is the God who wants me, broken and drowning in darkness, to go and serve. My God is the God of inside jokes, laughter, joy, and peacefulness. My God is the God that is so powerful he can change me from the inside, when I don't even really want him to. My God is so absolutely amazing that he would call me, by name, and send his son to die, just for me, his beloved.

In the army we are trained to always leave ourselves an exit. You never want to get caught in a place where you can't get out. I tried to give myself lots of exits in God's love, but he had me covered. I tried to walk away, run away, swim away, fly away, but I couldn't escape his crosshairs.

I believe my biggest battle is still ahead. I'm packing up and moving into a new chapter of my life, one that will inevitably involve my need to jump into serving a church in my hometown. When I went home after my military training, I avoided that old Baptist church like the plague. I attended four different churches in the four weeks I was home, sometimes driving hours just to go to them. But I knew, deep down, that one day I was going to have to walk back through the doors of that church that hurt me. That the biggest way that God should change me from the inside was to let me forgive them. To look them in the eye, shake their hands in that annoying time of greeting, and worship God with them.

God searches our hearts for the darkness, and when I think of returning to that Baptist church, my heart is full of darkness. But, he has shone his light onto it, and I know I need to humble myself, and instead of proudly telling them I've forgiven them, I need to ask them for forgiveness, and then worship with them.

I might even wear a red baseball cap when I do it.

Come As You Are
by David Crowder

Come out of sadness
From wherever you've been
Come broken hearted
Let rescue begin

Come find your mercy
Oh sinner come kneel
Earth has no sorrow
That heaven can't heal
Earth has no sorrow
That heaven can't heal

So lay down your burdens
Lay down your shame
All who are broken
Lift up your face
Oh Wanderer come home
You're not too far
So lay down your hurt
Lay down your heart
Come as you are

There's hope for the hopeless
And all those who've strayed
Come sit at the table
Come taste the grace
There's rest for the weary
Rest that endures
Earth has no sorrow
That heaven can't cure

So lay down your burdens
Lay down your shame
All who are broken
Lift up your face

Oh Wanderer come home, you're not too far...

Epilogue

My journey isn't complete. In fact, it's just getting started. I had to face that haunting question that I had deep down inside: "Is God really real?" And he showed me the answer. He came thundering into my life with undeniable power and glory. The least I can do is give my life to him.

One year after writing the bulk of this book I returned to the army for another summer of intense military training, this time in Gagetown, New Brunswick. As I faced the heavy burdens and challenges of military life, I was acutely aware that something was different from the summer before. This time around I *knew* that I wasn't doing it alone. I had this vision of God creating the universe, speaking the stars and sky into existence, and then all that power coming to rest in my heart. That the creator of the universe lives in me, and no matter what the army might throw at me, I can lean on the strength of God and I know that it will be enough. I'm constantly reminded of the verse in Psalms 18:30-34:

"As for God, his way is perfect: The Lord's word is flawless; he shields all who take refuge in him. For who is God besides the Lord? And who is the Rock except our God? It is God who arms me with strength and keeps my way secure. He makes my feet like the feet of a deer; he causes me to stand on the heights. He trains my hands for battle; my arms can bend a bow of bronze."

As the summer of training wore on, I began to search for my next adventure. I was faced with the decision of going back into coaching or continuing to work on the mission field. The original plan was that I would take one year off, walk the Camino, and then head to the mission field in Thailand, and afterwards take a coaching job and go on with life. However, as I began to search for a coaching job, it seemed that there wasn't much out there. I started to ask God if he could show me where he wanted me to go.

One last story: I have a friend, Tim, who is a pilot. Tim was telling me that when you need to come in to land the plane, you need to make sure there are three lights lined up on the runway. If there is only one or two lights, don't land, but if there are three, you're good to go. He told me that whenever he's trying to make a big decision, much like the runway lights, he looks for three things to line up. First, he looks for conviction, a burning or feeling deep down in his heart that he feels strongly about. The second thing he looks for is confirmation; does the decision line up with what God teaches in the Bible, or what he's trying to tell me? And finally, he looks for wise counsel from a friend or trusted advisor. If all three C's line up, then he knows what decision needs to be made.

As I was working through training in Gagetown, I made a new friend named Charles. We would walk to the gym together every day and discuss the events of the day, or just talk about life. I was starting to feel strongly that God was telling me to let go of my coaching career, or at least to hold it with an open hand. This was not easy to do. I had spent over a decade building this career, and much of my life and self-worth was based on my reputation as a hockey coach. It was terrifying to think about giving up that career. But if God wanted me to go back to Thailand, then I needed to listen. So I felt the conviction. Then one evening when Charles and I were walking, out of nowhere he said, "I think you should be a missionary." I started laughing; I couldn't believe the timing of his statement. I asked him why. He said, "I'm not sure; I just have this feeling like you should be on the mission field."

God will speak to us if we're ready to listen to him. If we get to know him, we'll hear his voice. And every time we hear it, it will fill our lives with so much joy, love, and peacefulness. I think maybe it's time to start living for my God instead of living for my job.

I have friends who say they "believe in God," but I've come to realize that just "believing in God" isn't good enough. Satan and his demons believe in God, but it doesn't mean they're going to get into heaven. God wants our hearts, and unfortunately too many people are going to miss heaven by twelve inches–the distance between their head and their heart. And then I have friends who will swear they're atheists. A few years ago I wouldn't have argued at all about the idea of atheism. I honestly wouldn't have really cared. But once I met God for who he *really is*, I can't for the life of me understand why anyone would want to believe we're all just a miscarriage of nature, rather than a perfectly loved creation.

As I come back to Christianity, and learn to walk a "Christian life," I revisit the rules, the traditions, and the religion that is all too often the focus. I've learned that God doesn't want us to follow rules; he just wants us to follow him. When I make choices now, I don't make them so I can follow the rules; instead, I make them because God deserves nothing less than the best I can give him. He deserves nothing less than coming to him with as pure a heart as possible, an honest life, and just giving him my best. If you haven't met that God, then you need to do it. He doesn't want you to be perfect; he's totally okay with brokenness. Just come as you are. Just talk to him and ask him to reveal himself to you.

If you're like me and grew up in a comfortable Christian

home–maybe it's time to rededicate your life to the one who created you. Maybe it's time to be all-in, to focus on relationship, and to laugh until you cry with Jesus. I promise you that you won't be disappointed.

God is great.

Acknowledgments

Most of this book was written in one sitting, in a Tim Horton's coffee shop just off the army base in Edmonton, Canada. The story and message hit me so hard that I knew I had to write it down, and once I started writing I couldn't stop. Through the process, there have been many people who deserve a shout out for their input, wisdom, and help. Jonathan, thanks for your wisdom, theological editing and for sharing your Nutella with me. Micha, thanks for your friendship, prayers, and wisdom. Liz, my editor, you do an outstanding job as always–I'm becoming a better writer each time I get a manuscript back from you. Mike, DJ, Katie, The CMCC Youth and the crew over at FBR–you guys became a family in such a short time and encouraged me more than you'd know.

For the people who are in this book, the people whose stories intertwine with mine. Your story is so full of joy and life, and I thank you for letting me be a part of it and for allowing me to share it. Rainer, my walking pal, thank you for your willingness to review and edit the book before print. Val, Mike my Polish friend, Jay, for your constant laughter and positive energy. Brett, for helping me to understand Jesus better. The entire Dion family, Dalton too, for welcoming me into your home, hearts, and lives. Pastor Greg and the Sturgeon Alliance family, I felt at home as soon as I walked in the doors.

My family, it's your unconditional love and support that allow me to live the crazy life I have; thank you. And finally, to the Keeper of Great Promise, I know who you are now, and I love you.

Want More?

Join the Mission: Dave continues to serve as a missionary overseas and relies on your generous donations to enable his work. Please consider becoming a giving partner. $1/day makes a big difference.

Want Dave to speak at your next event? Conference? Church service? Youth Event? Get in touch through his website.

Want to have coffee with Dave? He loves a good Italian cappuccino! Send an email through his blog to see where in the world he is, and if he's going to be in your area, he'd love to meet you!

Visit www.davidsmall.org for more

Preview of Nameless Faceless People

He waved the gun back and forth between my boss's face and mine. At the time I was calm; I was more surprised that despite all the tight security around the refugee camps, this man had snuck a gun in. It wasn't until days later that I realized he was 100% ready and willing to kill me. At that moment and in the moments afterward, it didn't occur to me that if this guy had gotten spooked, he would have taken my life. He had taken many lives; I wouldn't be the first—but maybe I'd be the first foreigner he'd kill.

My boss and I were possibly the first foreigners he had met in a long time. He had been in hiding for many years, slowly building an army. He was on terrorist watch lists, and every journalist I knew would kill to have an interview with him, but no one could find him. I hadn't believed we would get to meet with him until we walked into his compound a few minutes ago and he stepped out. From behind his back, he pulled a handgun and pointed it at us before placing it on the table.

After getting the call, I flew to Bangladesh to prepare for the meeting. I consulted with my boss, and he consulted with old friends who work in the FBI and State Department. One of our team members at headquarters put together a briefing binder with everything she could find about this guy and the army he was leading. I spent hours poring through anything I could find about ARSA, the Arakan Rohingya Salvation Army, and its leader.

He was born in Burma, a Rohingya himself. He moved to Saudi Arabia, where he grew up and studied to become an imam. After that, he went to Pakistan, where he studied guerrilla warfare tactics. Then he went back to Burma, where he started an army.

It was attacks by ARSA that led up to the ferocious Burma Army response of August 2017. ARSA killed six or seven Burma Army soldiers and afterwards just disappeared. The Burma Army was furious with these attacks and used them as an excuse to conduct genocide on the Rohingya people, attacking them with fury and disproportion, killing 10,000 men, women, and children. This led to a massive flight of the Rohingya people from Burma into Bangladesh. They streamed out as fast as they could, and by October over 800,000 Rohingya had fled from the steady, planned cleansing the Burma Army was conducting. Three weeks after the initial attacks, I stood in the middle of this sea of Rohingya refugees. And two years after that, I stood in front of one of the leaders of ARSA while he yelled in Arabic and waved a gun around.

When I arrived in Bangladesh to prepare for the meeting, we called our contact to let him know we were there. He asked where we'd be staying and said he would call us when the meeting was ready. We sat around the hotel for two days waiting. I assumed they were watching the hotel and watching us. We get spied on and followed quite a bit, but we had nothing to hide, so I figured it was okay if they wanted to observe us for a few days. After two days, we got the call. He said, "Rent a car tomorrow morning at 8 a.m. I want you driving north from your hotel along the Teknaf Road. I'll call you once you're on the road with more instructions." Then he hung up. Without us telling him, he already knew which hotel we were staying at, confirming my suspicions we were being watched.

As he'd instructed, we hired a car and, after a quick prayer, jumped in and started driving north at 8 a.m. sharp. We drove for about twenty minutes when the phone rang. It was our guy. He asked to speak to the driver. We passed the phone over, and the driver listened for a few minutes, said okay, and hung up. He turned the car around, drove back about a mile, and pulled over. An inconspicuous guy came over to our vehicle and, without knocking or saying anything, opened the side door and got in.

He looked just like any other Rohingya refugee who mills around the camp areas. Smiling at us, he shook our hands and began directing our driver. After guiding us for about ten minutes, he instructed our driver to pull over. Again, without saying anything, he opened the door, jumped out, and another guy jumped in. This guy repeated the same procedure. He shook our hands and guided the driver. We pulled off onto a tiny road that weaved through one of the refugee camps. These makeshift roads are barely wide enough for a vehicle to fit, and we were constantly brushing past people and refugee huts as we made our way through the overcrowded camp. He guided us as far as the road could take us, then we got out on foot.

There was another guy waiting for us. They handed us off, and the guy told us to follow him. He walked quickly through the trails that wound through the camp. It was a maze. We went down side roads, into someone's house, out the back door onto a little footpath. Back onto a main trail, around and in circles. After walking with us for about ten minutes, we met another guy at what I assumed was a predetermined meeting place.

These lower-ranking "foot soldiers" didn't know where the boss was hiding; they only knew enough to bring us to the next guy, who would know enough to bring us to the next guy. I think we were handed off five or six times. I could see they had a disciplined security plan in place as we made our way to meet the leader.

In the past, whenever I've been in the camps, I've been swarmed with people everywhere I go. Literally from the moment I step out of the vehicle, I'm surrounded by at least 20 or 30 people. And they follow me around. But this time it was different.

This time people would notice the white people walking, then they'd see who our guides were, and they would turn around and pretend like they hadn't noticed us. The refugees literally sit for hours on end in the doorway to their huts, and when we would pass with our guides, they would either turn around or go inside their houses, disappearing into the darkness. As we approached the compound where the boss would meet us, we got handed off three or four times within a few minutes and then ushered quickly into an enclosed compound with high walls. We were now way out at the back end of the refugee camp, where the camp butts up against the mountain range that runs like a spine down the Teknaf peninsula.

We were quickly ushered into the house and told to sit at a small table with plastic chairs around it. We sat and our latest guide disappeared into a back room. It wasn't more than a couple of minutes later that I was looking at the gun in the hand of the leader as he waved it around, proving to us that he was the real deal and that he was in charge.

It's a funny thing when someone is ready to kill you. It's funny—the thoughts that go through your mind and your reactions and instincts that kick in. Many people talk about our response to fear by activating the "fight or flight" response—but some people also freeze. They don't run away (flight) and they don't pounce (fight); they freeze in a place of total uselessness. It's like their muscles turn to cement and, despite their brains trying to talk some sense into them, they're stuck. I've seen this unfold in people.

But at this moment, when I had a gun waving in my face, I found my thoughts wondering how on earth did I wander into this situation? What choices in my life led me to this moment?

About the Author

David Small comes from the small town of Kenora, Ontario, Canada where he loves spending the summer on the lake and running away at the first sign of fall approaching. David now calls Chiang Mai, Thailand his home. He is the author of *The Wandering Leader*, *The Hope Project*, *Small Stories*, and *Nameless Faceless People*. He also wrote and produced the soundtrack to Nameless Faceless People available on Spotify.

David is currently the director of the Jungle Discipleship School in Burma and co-owner of Apex Fitness in Chiang Mai. David served for ten years in the Canadian Army Reserves where he reached the rank of Captain. He has a bachelor of science degree from Haaga-Helia University of Science in Vierumaki, Finland, but Finland was too cold for him.

He welcomes your emails if you want to send him a personal message: dave@jungledisipleshipschool.com

instagram.com/jungledisipleshipschool
facebook.com/jungledisipleshipschool
youtube.com/jungledisipleshipschool

Publishing Books That Matter

WRITERS:
We publish courageous, meaningful stories that refuse to be forgettable.
If you have a manuscript that matters, we want to read it.

READERS:
Discover books that value truth, craft, adventure and the long road of faith.
Follow us to find your next great read.

www.SmallRevolutionPublishing.com

www.ingramcontent.com/pod-product-compliance
Lightning Source LLC
Chambersburg PA
CBHW020418080526
44584CB00014B/1387